Cambridge Elements

Elements in New Religious Movements
Series Editor
Rebecca Moore
San Diego State University
Founding Editor
†James R. Lewis
Wuhan University

MAKING PLACES SACRED

New Articulations of Place and Power

Matt Tomlinson
Australian National University

Yujie Zhu
Australian National University

CAMBRIDGE
UNIVERSITY PRESS

Shaftesbury Road, Cambridge CB2 8EA, United Kingdom

One Liberty Plaza, 20th Floor, New York, NY 10006, USA

477 Williamstown Road, Port Melbourne, VIC 3207, Australia

314–321, 3rd Floor, Plot 3, Splendor Forum, Jasola District Centre, New Delhi – 110025, India

103 Penang Road, #05–06/07, Visioncrest Commercial, Singapore 238467

Cambridge University Press is part of Cambridge University Press & Assessment, a department of the University of Cambridge.

We share the University's mission to contribute to society through the pursuit of education, learning and research at the highest international levels of excellence.

www.cambridge.org
Information on this title: www.cambridge.org/9781009616324
DOI: 10.1017/9781009616355

© Matt Tomlinson and Yujie Zhu 2025

This publication is in copyright. Subject to statutory exception and to the provisions of relevant collective licensing agreements, no reproduction of any part may take place without the written permission of Cambridge University Press & Assessment.

When citing this work, please include a reference to the DOI 10.1017/9781009616355

First published 2025

A catalogue record for this publication is available from the British Library

ISBN 978-1-009-61632-4 Hardback
ISBN 978-1-009-61631-7 Paperback
ISSN 2635-232X (online)
ISSN 2635-2311 (print)

Cambridge University Press & Assessment has no responsibility for the persistence or accuracy of URLs for external or third-party internet websites referred to in this publication and does not guarantee that any content on such websites is, or will remain, accurate or appropriate.

Making Places Sacred

New Articulations of Place and Power

Elements in New Religious Movements

DOI: 10.1017/9781009616355
First published online: March 2025

Matt Tomlinson
Australian National University

Yujie Zhu
Australian National University

Author for correspondence: Matt Tomlinson, matt.tomlinson@anu.edu.au

Abstract: Although claims to sacredness are often linked to the power of a distant past, the work of making places sacred is creative, novel, renewable, and reversible. This Element highlights how sacred space is newly made. It is often associated with blood, death, and geographic anomalies, yet no single feature determines sacred associations. People make space sacred by connecting with "extrahuman" figures – the ancestors, spirits, and gods that people attempt to interact with in every society. These connections can be concentrated in people's bodies, yet bodies are particularly vulnerable to loss. The Element also examines the multidimensional and multisensory dimensions of sacred space, which can be made almost anywhere, including online, but can also be unmade. Unmaking sacred space can entail new sacralization. New and minority religions in particular provide excellent sites for studying sacredness as a value, raising the reliably productive question: sacred for whom?

This Element also has a video abstract: Cambridge.org/ENRM_Tomlinson

Keywords: sacred places, sacred space, new religious movements, ritual, spirituality

© Matt Tomlinson and Yujie Zhu 2025

ISBNs: 9781009616324 (HB), 9781009616317 (PB), 9781009616355 (OC)
ISSNs: 2635-232X (online), 2635-2311 (print)

Contents

Introduction	1
1 Sacred for Whom?	2
2 Blood and Death Make Places Sacred	10
3 Natural Features and the Sacred	14
4 Performing the Sacred	18
5 The Body – the Most Vulnerable Sacred Site	27
6 Sacred Space Is Multidimensional	32
7 Sacred Space Is Multisensory	37
8 Sacred Space Can Be Unmade	42
9 Sacred Space Reaffirms the Human	46
Conclusion	51
References	53

Introduction

In this Element, we analyze sacred space: what it is, how people make it and use it, and the limits of sacralization. The discussion that follows is arranged as a sequence of nine related points. We discuss our reasoning and give examples in each section.

Perhaps counterintuitively, our grounding argument is that no universal statement about sacred space is sustainable. In stating this, we do not claim originality, as Jonathan Z. Smith made the case cogently decades ago. He wrote, "there is nothing that is inherently sacred or profane. These are not substantive categories, but rather situational ones. Sacrality is, above all, a category of emplacement" (Smith, 1987: 104). We follow Smith's reasoning and expand the concept of emplacement to include bodies, senses, and the virtual world. We also draw on his description in that same work of ritual as "a mode of paying attention," analyzing sacred space as something such attention produces (Smith, 1987: 103).

We define the sacred as the connection between humanity and "extrahuman" figures – the ghosts, reanimated ancestors, nature spirits, gods, and souls that people attempt to interact with in some form in every society. Sacred space is made different from regular (or "profane") space in its articulation with loss and memory (for example, in memorials to the dead), reverence (in worship), fear (in taboo restrictions), and fortune (in expressions of *mana*, spiritual power, blessing and luck). In setting this frame for our exploration, we might seem to be building a universal argument, but in the following pages we will keep the focus on the partiality of understandings of sacred space: your sacred space might not be mine, and vice versa. Moreover, scholars should keep the category of regular/profane open and active. Some spaces are plainly *not* sacred for most people, but the reasons for their non-sacredness are not always evident, and repay consideration.

New Religious Movements (NRMs) are ideal social contexts for the creation of new sacred space. Because NRMs often stand at a critical angle to mainstream religious groups, sanctifying physical points of reference can help ground NRMs' fresh claims and innovative practices.

Consider the example of Spiritualism. In this movement, mediums attempt to connect listeners with spirits of their loved ones. It emerged historically from American Christianity as inflected by Swedenborgianism, Mesmerism, and the writings of Andrew Jackson Davis (1826–1910). In the following pages, we will give examples of the various ways Spiritualist mediums make places sacred, including their own bodies. Here, we note that as the movement became institutionalized in regional and national organizations, particular places have become identified with effective spirit mediumship. Spiritualists in Australia treat the Arthur Findlay College in Stansted Mountfitchet, England, as a sacred site. The college, located on the same grounds as the United Kingdom's Spiritualists' National Union, is considered the most prestigious training ground for Spiritualist mediums in the world. It holds classes year-round on spirit mediumship and psychic work, training opportunities for which Australian mediums are eager to travel across the globe. It is a site where metaphysical theory is put into practice (see, e.g., Kalvig, 2017: 94–6 on a memorable table-tipping séance there). For many Spiritualists in the United States, the hallowed ground is Lily Dale, a village in upstate New York which is home to the National Spiritualist Association of Churches. To own a home in Lily Dale, you must be a member of the local Spiritualist governing body (the Assembly). Thousands of people visit the village in summer for its workshops and for private sessions with mediums (Wicker, 2003). One could look more closely at particular sites within these locations – for example, the tombstone of famed medium Emma Hardinge Britten at the Arthur Findlay College, or the Inspiration Stump at Lily Dale, where mediums give readings in a forest clearing. Our point is simply that by establishing sites like the Arthur Findlay College and the village of Lily Dale, Anglophone Spiritualists have declared that they offer something different: new grounds for engaging with the spirit world here and now.

In this Element, we turn to NRMs for many examples of sacred space-making. We acknowledge that mainstream religious institutions also work energetically at defining sacred space, sometimes in their own novel ways. Thus, in focusing on "the newness of sacred space," we emphasize that the newness is in the practice and not only in the movement or institution.

Please note, we use the terms "space" and "place" interchangeably, although we realize that some readers would prefer to reserve "space" for physical area in general and "place" for specific locations made meaningful by human action and interpretation.

1 Sacred for Whom?

In February 2023, Matt Tomlinson conducted an interview in Canberra, Australia, with two spirit mediums, a married couple named Norman and Lynette Ivory. Matt had known them for more than seven years, and understood a bit about their philosophy of life and visions of the spirit world. He had taken a course on mediumship, which they taught when they were the leaders of the Canberra Spiritualist Association.

On this day, Norman surprised Matt with his recollection of seeing an archangel. The main topic of the interview was spirit healing. Late in the discussion, talk had turned to the subject of angels, and Lynette said that angels have different responsibilities: "You've got angels of love, angels of healing, angels of war ... every emotion you can think of, there's an angelic force involved." Norman lamented that Spiritualists do not understand as much about angels as they used to. He then added that he and Lynette "have experience with angels," and proceeded to describe the time they went to "a little park by the side of the railway." He was not sure where it had been. Lynette suggested Bundanoon, a town around 150 kilometers from Sydney. "Bundanoon sounds right," Norman agreed. "We sat in this little park right next to the railway, not too far from the railway station in Bundanoon, and an archangel came. An archangel is quite big. This is not a small being. This is quite a tall being. This angel would have been twenty feet high at least."

He mentioned that "A host of angels will have an archangel in charge," and returned to his critique of Spiritualists' diminished understanding of angels today. Matt steered the interview back to the park: "Can I ask what happened then in that park in Bundanoon? Was there a message, or was there – "

"Well, he came and he talked through me," Norman replied, patiently. "He talked to us both, talked about what we were doing, where we were going in Spiritualism. He also – did he talk about the family?"

"I've got no idea, darling," Lynette said. "I don't remember."

"I can't remember," Norman mused, and added, "That's something that [his spirit guide] Sun Tsen would usually talk to me about. It was basically philosophical and based ... [on] what was going on as far as Spiritualism was concerned in our lives. Because we were then running the Hills Spiritualist Centre, and obviously that was a fairly successful church."

Norman often sees spiritual beings. In the first of his three books, *The Rabbit on the Roof*, he tells of many vivid encounters: meeting hundreds of dancing fairies; seeing the bird-headed angel of death in a friend's room at the hospital; meeting a kind but cautious elf while walking in the woods; and banishing a "piglike imp" that had been afflicting a household, for example (Ivory, 2016: 217, 222, 238, 180–2). Yet the archangel story still surprised Matt. Note how the event was memorable, but the place less so, and the message even less. An archangel, in Norman's description, is not just another spirit being. It is an especially large one, pulsing with extraordinary energy. Nevertheless, after one appeared to Norman and spoke through him, the words faded from memory, and he needed prompting from Lynette to remember that it was in Bundanoon. An extraordinary messenger had delivered a routine message in what might seem an unremarkable place.

If one actively seeks spiritual visions, one might be expected to head to the usual places: majestic shrines, ancient houses, deep forests, the edge of the sea. Even the militant atheist Richard Dawkins (2004: 137) admits to being

Figure 1 Bundanoon seen from its train station platform, August 2, 2024. Photo by Matt Tomlinson.

moved by the profound depth of the Grand Canyon, although he grumpily deflects his emotions onto his reader and retreats into the passive voice: "Why, when you go to the Grand Canyon and you see the strata of geological time laid out before you, why ... is there a feeling that brings you close to tears?" A park next to a rail line in a small town, by comparison, might not be high on many people's lists of spiritually magnetic places. Matt did find Norman's story intriguing, however, and paid a visit to Bundanoon in August 2024 (see Figure 1).

Putting aside the element of surprise, it is worthwhile to ask how other scholars might respond to Norman's story. Some readers might hark back to Mircea Eliade's classic work (1961) on ritual and characterize Norman's experience as a hierophany, a moment when the sacred appears to humans and establishes the connection which centers humanity in the world and enables communication with the divine. Others, agreeing with Jonathan Z. Smith (1987) on Eliade's analytic limitations, might say that Norman had actively made the park sacred with his vision, "paying attention" in a ritualized way wherein his interests transformed a seemingly ordinary space. He sacralized the park by seeing it anew. In doing so, he prompted Matt to go there to pay attention to it with heightened interest.

As Smith writes, the sacred is "above all, a category of emplacement" (1987: 104). A casual visitor might not encounter the sacred in Bundanoon, but Norman did, and Lynette did through Norman's experience. Matt went there and enjoyed it, but did not see anything out of the ordinary. Their experiences understandably diverge from Aboriginal visions of it as a place inhabited by kin for tens of thousands of years.

Even as no space is inherently sacred, some places obviously earn a reputation for spiritual efficacy: Mecca. Lourdes. The Ganges River. Indeed, some sites become such powerful icons of sacredness that the idea of newly or differently sacralized places can sit uneasily alongside them. The British journalist Hannen Swaffer, a committed Spiritualist, groused that even after mediums presented incontrovertible proof of life after death, audiences stubbornly rejected it: "You do not accept evidence of the hereafter like that, even if you accept it when you read the New Testament, concerning the writing of which you know nothing whatever. It must take place in Jerusalem to convince you, not Kingston Vale" (Swaffer, 1962: 5). Many people expect the sacred in Jerusalem in a way they do not in Kingston Vale – or Bundanoon – and although stating this fact baldly may seem to belabor the obvious, we suggest drawing back to ask why and how, culturally speaking, this is the case.

Can an entire country be sacred? Here, we are not referring to places like Israel or Vatican City, but to places that most visitors would not consider sacred, but many locals do. In an earlier research project, Matt conducted fieldwork at Christian theological colleges in Sāmoa and American Sāmoa. The independent nation of Sāmoa is possibly the most Christian country in the world, demographically speaking. In 2013, an estimated 98.8 percent of its population belonged to a Christian church (Grim, Johnson, Skirbekk, and Zurlo, 2014: 38). A legal scholar declares that Sāmoa is not technically a Christian state, but is a de facto one because Christianity thoroughly shapes national self-understandings and works its way into key texts such as the national motto ("Sāmoa is founded on God"), the Constitution (whose preamble states that "sovereignty over the Universe belongs to the Omnipresent God alone"), and the national anthem (which includes the line, "God is our foundation, our freedom"; Ahdar, 2013). The theologian Ama'amalele Tofaeono writes of pre-Christian Sāmoa as literally Edenic, a place where humans interacted with all of living creation in a holistically interconnected and fundamentally sacred way. But he adds that the arrival of Christian missionaries ruined things, changing Sāmoa from an inherently sacred place in tune with God's will into one alienated from the natural order (Tofaeono, 2000).

In short, many Sāmoans see the nation as godly, even if they do not agree on how to evaluate the work of European missionaries (see also Efi, 2014).

Now consider another perspective, that of an Englishman named Donald Hemingway, who became obsessed in the early 1950s about God's mission for him. Hemingway heard God speak often and at length, although he wrote that he was "not a person given to imagination or hallucination" (Hemingway, 1993: 72). God's message to Hemingway became direct and urgent one day at Richmond, in Surrey:

> It was on Saturday morning, 7th April 1951, after nine months of prayer and waiting upon the Lord that my prayers were to be answered. Leaving home at the usual time of 7.30 am I was halfway down the Upper Richmond Road, cycling fast and yet waiting upon the Lord when, like a bolt out of the blue, the one word SAMOA was given to me. I heard it distinctly. I said, "Lord what is it, what does it mean, is it a person's name or is it a place?" Then I remembered that the night before I had been to a farewell service of a friend of the family who was leaving as a missionary for Africa. I wondered if this could be a place she had mentioned. All the rest of the way to the store this one word SAMOA was ringing in my ears and kind of hitting me on the head like a hammer. It seemed impossible to work that morning.... I was very [per CMS 12.62, 18th ed.] thankful when 1 o'clock came and my lunch hour. Rushing from the shop with "Samoa" still ringing in my ears, I made my way down the High Street into W. H. Smith's large bookshop, one of London's noted booksellers. It was full of people and I had to push my way in. Eventually I was able to pick up an atlas. Turning to the map of Africa I began to look all over to see if I would see a place ... called Samoa. Not finding what I wanted I suddenly heard a voice say, "Why don't you turn to the index." I thought how stupid of me not to have done this at the beginning. Turning to the index I read "Samoan Islands, Pacific Ocean." I then said, "Thank you Lord, I believe this must be the place where you want me to go." As soon as I said those words, the ringing and the hammering of the word "Samoa" in my ears and heart ceased and a wonderful peace and joy stole over my whole being. This was the first time in my life that I understood there was such a place in existence called Samoa. For the rest of that day I seemed to walk on air. (Hemingway, 1993: 12)

Later, on September 15, 1952, on the isle of Guernsey, he was praying when he received a vision of a thatched-roof home standing between palm trees, and "the Lord audibly spoke and said, 'I will give thee the heathen for thine inheritance'" (Hemingway, 1993: 16, quoting Psalms 2:8).

On one level, this is a moving story of faith and the search for sacred space. Hemingway is hit hard by what he takes to be God's words, determined to understand the significance of that mysterious word "Samoa," and feeling like he is walking "on air" when he understands where his new mission is to take place. On another level, it is the story of someone who stumbles off the path trying to find what is right in front of him. Carrying out what he believed to be his divine mission, Hemingway arrived in Tutuila, American Sāmoa, on

November 7, 1956, ready for those heathen. In his book, he carries on with his narrative as we might expect, full of fervor and determination to outmaneuver his opponents. But despite learning the basics of Sāmoan mission history and acknowledging that everyone goes to church, he never quite comes out and admits that in looking for the heathen, the Christian missionary had arrived at the most Christian place on earth.

As it happened, the same year he arrived, a census was taken in American Sāmoa and the proportion of the population recorded as Christian was at least 95 percent; it was probably higher, because the category "Other" (998 persons, out of a total population of 20,154) almost certainly included Christians not counted in the main denominations. Yet for someone like Donald Hemingway, the people in Sāmoa could never be Christian enough, because they were not enough like him. They went to church regularly, but not religiously, because real religion for Hemingway was a distinct brand of Pentecostalism. His theology and anthropology were like an overfocused beam of light that, passing the point of fineness, becomes blurry again.

Although Hemingway's story does have its humorous aspects, we retell it not to make fun of him, but rather to point out that he agreed fully with many Sāmoans on the divine significance of Sāmoa. He just saw it from a completely different angle – one that, to others' eyes, might seem to distort the situation into unrecognizability.

To put the matter as a question: *Is Sāmoa a sacred place?* Everyone agrees: Yes, it is. National discourse proclaims Sāmoa's divine foundation. The theologian Ama'amalele Tofaeono portrays pre-Christian Sāmoa as united with God's purpose. The missionary Donald Hemingway also felt Sāmoa had been chosen by God, although his understanding of his mission might jar Sāmoan sensibilities. We can widen this range of perspectives, too, as there are non-Christian sacred sites in Sāmoa such as the Baha'i temple, set on lush grounds high on the mountain over which the Cross Island Road runs (see Figure 2).

We are not claiming that any place is sacred just because someone says it is. It might be sacred for one person but not another, or sacred for many people for different reasons. This assertion might sound obvious to the point of banality. But it is always worth making, if only to remind ourselves that sacredness is a value, and that as a value it is always open to reevaluation.

The variable evaluation of sacredness is exemplified in an earlier research project by Yujie Zhu, who conducted fieldwork in Yunnan province in Southwest China, where various forms of religious folk culture have historically fused and intertwined. One significant indigenous folk religion of the region, Dongba, originates from the Tibetan Bon tradition (Mu, 1995; Li, 1997; Yang, 2008; Xu, 2023). Following the Cultural Revolution (1966–1976), Dongba and many folk

Figure 2 Baha'i Temple, Upolu, Sāmoa, April 26, 2015. Photo by Matt Tomlinson.

religious practices in this region, as in other parts of the country, were destroyed or forbidden (Chao, 1995, 2012; Mu, 1995; McKhann, 2010). Consequently, very few practitioners maintained the knowledge for ritual practices in the villages.

Since the 1980s, however, the local government has promoted tourism for local development, aiming to satisfy especially Western imaginations of the area as an "Oriental" paradise (Rees, 2000; McKhann, 2010; Zhu 2018).[1] In this process, Dongba practices and their associated culture have been packaged as exotic folk

---

[1] Joseph Rock (1947) and Peter Goullart (1955) depicted Lijiang as a distant, nostalgic "magic kingdom." Building on their descriptions, documentaries like Phil Agland's *China: Beyond the Clouds* (1994) perpetuate the mythology of Lijiang as an exotic and secluded region, a notion that captivated early Western visitors and was further popularized in guidebooks such as Lonely Planet (Su and Teo, 2009). For more extensive discussions on this topic, see works including

religion to satisfy these imaginations (Blum, 2001; Chen, 2014). The Tibetan shamanic ritual of Dongba has been romanticized, staged, and sometimes shortened for the heritage tourism industry (Cohen, 1988; Zhu, 2018), with modern performances mostly treated as mass entertainment for the tourist industry.

While most tourists and local communities treat these performances as commercial products, some Dongba practitioners still regard certain rituals, particularly those conducted for their own families and villages, as sacred and efficacious (Cohen, 1988; Mathieu, 2003; Yang, 2008; Zhu, 2012, 2018). Meanwhile, local scholars, primarily trained ethnologists, are conducting research on ancient Dongba scriptures as a way to categorize and reconnect with local indigenous culture (Li, 1997: 200–11; Chao, 2012: 57–8). For these scholars, the sacred originates from their association with indigenous thoughts, knowledge, and cosmology (Mu, 1995: 58–9). This differs from practitioners' perceptions of sacredness, which are more associated with their capacity to connect with nature through ritual practices (Chao, 2012). As demonstrated here, the sacred can differ in the same site for people with different purposes at different times (see Figure 3).

Figure 3 A Dongba wedding ritual for a newly married couple in Lijiang, February 2011. Photo by Yujie Zhu.

McKhann (1992), Mathieu (2003), and Arcones (2012), as well as Naxi researchers such as Mu (1995) and Yang (2008).

If no universal claim about sacred space is possible, as we are arguing, there are nonetheless effective tools for analyzing particular claims about particular places. Charles S. Peirce's classic semiotic distinction between an icon (a sign which signifies by resemblance), an index (which signifies by connection), and a symbol (which signifies by convention) is useful to bear in mind. Although most signs have combined iconic, indexical, and symbolic force for interpreters, the relative emphasis varies. In examining sacred space, many observers get caught on the iconic part – for example, ancestors say this mountain range is a sleeping goddess because the landform roughly resembles a reclining woman. But the most significant relationship for defining and engaging with sacred space is usually the indexical force in which people assert a connection between an object – that mountain range, this body; that statue, this nation – and an existentially different character or quality this connection brings into the world.

2 Blood and Death Make Places Sacred

Blood can sanctify or pollute. When it spills into the ground, it can mark places as sites of violence and loss, hence possible memorialization and recuperation. Perhaps the most active and visible project of sacred placemaking in Australia and the United States is the proliferation of roadside memorials to those killed in accidents. Chances are that readers have seen these micro-monuments while driving – crosses popping out of weeds and cut flowers lying incongruously on embankments, mute announcements that somebody died here.

Holly Everett (2002) has noted that placing roadside crosses to mark fatalities is a practice older and more widespread than one might suspect. Several authors trace the practice to Mexico and the southwestern United States, with one even claiming that roadside crosses are "perhaps one of the few authentic non-commercial folk arts of New Mexico's Hispanics" (Estevan Arrellano quoted in Barrera, 1991: 279; see also Henzel, 1991; Collins and Rhine, 2003). Memorials can evolve over time, as simple wooden crosses placed when grief is raw might be replaced later with more ornate, durable, and personalized objects (Collins and Rhine, 2003: 232). There are cultural variations in style and emphasis. For example, the authors of a study of roadside memorials in Newcastle, New South Wales, Australia, characterized them as monuments to machismo and aggression (Hartig and Dunn, 1998), whereas Dutch scholars have written of such memorials in the Netherlands symbolizing "victimhood, vulnerability, transitoriness, innocence and tenderness" (Klaassens, Groote, and Huigen, 2009: 191).[2] Roadside memorials are often intended to keep alive

---

[2] The authors of the Australian study were so irritated by the sentiments expressed by memorials' creators that they advised an ad agency working on a road-safety campaign that "roadside

Figure 4 Roadside memorial cross, Fairbairn Avenue, Canberra, June 10, 2024. Photo by Matt Tomlinson.

a social connection with the deceased person (see Figure 4), a way of avoiding saying "goodbye" and instead "suggest[ing] a desire to 'not let go'" (Collins and Rhine, 2003: 228). In some cultural contexts, however, the living connection can be distinctly unwelcome. Koyi Mchunu (2020: 8) observes that "In Ghana, the general belief is that erecting a roadside death memorial for a beloved would be tantamount to encouraging/inviting such incidents to occur in one's life."

Bodies, their sites of death, and memorials to them do not need to be connected in space, however. One of Benedict Anderson's key observations in his landmark work *Imagined Communities* (1983) was that Tombs of Unknown Soldiers are powerful precisely because the identity of the dead soldier has dissolved. The body is brought back within national borders and honored in a place it did not fall, and the disarticulation of body, death site, and memorial actually enhances the emotional power of the site: this anonymous soldier could be anyone, their death is yours and ours, because the nation eternally needs you to defend it. In being labelled memorials by their designers, these sites enable new connections with the dead, setting up indexes of both physical loss and the possibility of recuperation. For example, writing about the Vietnam Veterans Memorial in Washington, DC, Robert Pogue Harrison describes the reactions it

---

memorials would only have utility as road safety messages aimed at young men if they came to be seen as a condemnation rather than glorification of problematic hyper-masculinity" (Hartig and Dunn, 1998: 19).

provokes: "The irresistible need many visitors feel to touch a chiseled name, kiss it, talk to it, offer it flowers or gifts, leave it notes or letters, is evidence enough of the dead's privative presence in the stone – a presence at once given and denied" (2003: 137). Soldiers reassemble as names on a wall, read and cherished and mourned by the living, eight thousand miles from where they fell and are now remembered and recognized again.

Sites can be marked as sacred when people recall those who lived there, however they may have died. When Matt conducted fieldwork in Kadavu Island, Fiji, he encountered the reanimated presence of the dead at an ancient village site. There was nothing scary about it, but for the young woman who led him and another young man to the old village in April 1999, the visitors needed to affirm their respect. The group had gone there to gather red ginger as decorations for village festivities. Upon arriving at the site, the woman said aloud (in Fijian), "Good morning [polite phrasing]. We request flowers." When passing an old foundation, she said "Excuse me" several times, the same way she would have if living humans had been sitting there. When leaving the site, she said, "Thanks for the flowers." Other than her words, the place was quiet and still. Her words revealed her sense that the ancestors still lived there metaphysically, and deserved the respectful recognition they would have received when physically alive (see Tomlinson, 2009: 138–9).

Harrison states that "The surest way to take possession of a place and secure it as one's own is to bury one's dead in it" (2003: 24). He extends this argument to the United States as a polity: the US Constitution does not effectively "ground" the nation, which only dead bodies can do. He thus turns to Abraham Lincoln's Gettysburg Address, wherein soldiers' bodies are credited with sacralizing the ground so that the nation might live: "we cannot dedicate, we cannot consecrate – we cannot hallow – this ground. The brave men, living and dead, who struggled here, have consecrated it far above our poor power to add or detract." Harrison then goes a step further and characterizes Lincoln's murder as a sacrifice.

His claim may be overstated.[3] But to work with the idea nevertheless, it is useful to consider cemeteries' status as sacred spaces. Cemeteries visibly and publicly articulate death, and often at large scale. Obviously, the ways people use the space vary widely. Mourners at a burial are often sorrowful and reverential; teenagers getting high at night in the graveyard and tipping over the headstones, not so much. So, are cemeteries sacred spaces? As with every

---

[3] After claiming that burial of the dead is the "surest" technique of ownership, Harrison acknowledges that "Not all cultures mark the graves of their ancestors, to be sure, or assert proprietary rights over the land through burial of their dead" (2003: 24). Such conviction on opposing sides of an argument exemplifies the truth that you cannot lose a debate if you take both sides.

either/or question we pose in this Element, the answer is an unashamed and resolute "It depends."

To approach the matter historically, it bears mention that particular cemeteries' social status can change significantly over time. Thomas Harvey, studying graveyards in Portland, Oregon, observes seemingly paradoxical historical transformations. In the nineteenth century, town planners rarely included cemeteries as urban features, partly because they were seen as "potential health hazards" and because they would not provide tax revenue (Harvey, 2006: 295–6). They were established on city outskirts, on cheap land. As cities expanded, those outlying graveyards were outlying no more, but right within the suburbs, and the land they were on was no longer cheap. In the nineteenth century, developers did sometimes relocate cemeteries, but relocation became rarer in the twentieth century as cemeteries became historical sites in their own right and valued as scarce green space, even wildlife habitats – when not being feared as toxic waste sites full of cadaver-preserving formaldehyde (Olson, 2016).

Cemeteries can be dedicated to the dead they hold in different ways, by which we mean that some cemeteries are planned as sacred sites of reverence and memory, and other cemeteries are planned as profane sites for forgetting or insulting the dead. After an attempted coup in Turkey in 2016, the government established a cemetery in Istanbul for traitors, and the mayor proclaimed it an ideal site to "curse and humiliate the graves of coup-affiliated soldiers" (Zengin, 2019: 94). Asli Zengin tells the haunting stories of Turkish transgender women who face dilemmas about where their bodies and those of their loved ones will be buried. Cemeteries for the "unknown" hold the remains of homeless people, refugees, and victims of police brutality. The family of one transgender woman, Ayşe, specifically asked the state to bury her in a cemetery for the unknown, a final act of disavowal in Ayşe's tragic life (93). One of Ayşe's friends, Ceyda, is so worried about the possibility of ending up in a cemetery for the unknown that she plans to have her body donated to a medical school (94).

At sites ranging from humble roadside markers to massive constructions like the Vietnam Veterans Memorial, then, blood and death often index a place's sacredness. But not all sites of violence or death become sacred, and the people who develop and visit these sites can have widely divergent understandings of why and how *this* site deserves special attention and treatment. For example, Elizabeth L. Greenspan (2006) writes that the creation of the 9/11 memorial site in Manhattan was roughly shaped by competing interests among government officials, developers, urban planners, architects, and designers. Different groups held clashing opinions. Noting that "questions of scale are often integral to politics of memorialization," Greenspan observes how homemade tributes left at the site were prohibited lest they imply that this place was essentially public – a sentiment that sat uneasily alongside plans to develop significant new commercial properties there (257–8). Yet attempts to make the memorial tell a story that went beyond America, a narrative that included global struggles for freedom, were also actively opposed. What ultimately emerged at the 9/11 memorial was markedly American nationalist sacredness, and many voices were erased in the construction of it.

"Although death is the great universal," Katherine Verdery writes (1999: 22; see also Engelke, 2021), "it calls forth human responses that are extraordinarily varied. The fact that people are everywhere digging up and reburying other people does not mean that all those instances have the same sense." Likewise, sacred spaces are extraordinarily varied, indeed almost infinitely so. But the contingencies that make spaces sacred can come to seem determinative and obvious. Blood and death do not automatically make any place sacred, but they are common resources for people's marking, thinking about, and fighting over spaces as sacred.

3 Natural Features and the Sacred

Some places have features that seem naturally to suggest sacredness. A mountain presents an immensity so far beyond human scale that it can be both entirely visible and impossible to grasp at the same time. A forest of towering trees leads eyes upward to ever more life. A rolling sea seems both ever-changing and eternal. Thomas F. Gieryn describes such associations evocatively when he writes, "There is something compelling about particular locations, the materials encrusted there, the stories told about the place." One example he offers is Delphi, in Greece, with a "spectacular landscape [that] has always been remarkable, and for that reason it has never been unnarrated" (2018: 4, 171–2; see also Manning, 2017).

But trying to theorize from this basis becomes hazardous, a trap of logical circularity: this place is sacred because it looks like that, and looking like that is what makes it sacred. Such reasoning usually cannot identify a causal connection between appearance (looking "like" something, a subjective judgment of what counts as iconic) and response (inferring sacredness, asserting an indexical connection between this place and its extraordinary existential qualities). Gieryn's shorthand phrase, "something compelling," covers a lot of semiotic territory and interpretive work.

Nonetheless, some places are so different from everything around them that people tend to agree that they stand apart. Japanese citizens describe Mount Osore as "weird," "mysterious," and "creepy" (*bukimi, fushigi, kimiwarui*), a literally dreadful place (Ivy, 1995: 163). It is a remote volcanic mountain cloaked in cypress, with stony ground and a sulfurous blue lake in its crater; Marilyn Ivy calls it a "topography of death," foreboding and bleak (141–4). Japanese citizens see it as a place where spirits of the dead can be both placated and stirred up, settled through memorialization and called back by blind women shamans. Visitors buy memorial stupas made of wood, take loved ones' ashes to an ossuary, and make offerings of flowers, candy, money, and especially stones to miniature statues of Jizō, the site's principal Buddhist deity. In doing so, they explicitly mark a place whose terrain is overdetermined as eerie – rugged, remote, stony, sulfurous – as truly a site of death. Ivy even refers to the mountain fancifully as a "metagraveyard," a general and comprehensive site for the dead (154). The temple complex "resembles a frontier outpost ... the terrain itself overshadows its managing institution" (142). The landscape is so otherworldly that for Japanese visitors, it makes perfect sense that here is where the dead go.

Rather than look for a firm indexical-iconic connection between a landscape's features and what kinds of spirits, gods, and other extrahuman beings might live there, we suggest it can be more fruitful to think of the ways in which landscapes serve as sites in which wonder – an openness to amazement – finds points on which to focus. Michael W. Scott analyzes the ways Arosi people of Makira Island, Solomon Islands, describe astonishing things like strange aircraft flying above, unexplained lights shining below the ocean's surface, and "large mechanical whales and porpoises crewed by unknown humans" (2016: 486). Scott argues that these phenomena are indexical signs of a major ontological shift in Arosi society. In their traditional understandings, Arosi were descendants of beings who were essentially separate in origin, such as a snake, a bird, or a *kakamora*, a spiritually powerful dwarflike creature. These beings' matrilineal descendants are entirely human but also foundationally different from each other; each matriline is "consubstantial with a particular area of land.... To belong to the ... matrilineage of a particular territory is to exist in continuity of being with that land" (481). Arosi ontology has begun to shift, however, and they increasingly consider themselves to be foundationally united as Makira Islanders.

Scott identifies three reasons for this shift. One is latent in an origin myth that tells of a giant snake that made the island fertile but left after its daughter's husband, unaware of who the snake was, attacked it. The man chopped up the snake, so it re-formed its body and left Makira for another island. This story might seem to suggest an original unity for Makirans, but Scott notes that Arosi do not fully endorse this reasoning (2016: 481–2; see also Scott, 2007). In addition, they have embraced Christianity, which has entailed the flattening of diverse practices into a presumed "common core *kastom* [custom] said to be consonant with Christianity," a way of maintaining that Arosi had not needed white people to show up to teach them about God (2016: 483; compare Tofaeono, 2000). Finally, and most forcefully, the Solomon Islands' civil war from 1998 to 2003 led many Arosi to see themselves as united against a threat from stereotypically warlike Malaitan Islanders. United by an external threat, Arosi have come to consider themselves – seemingly gentle, vulnerable, and poor – as custodians of an immense spiritual power.

The strange things appearing on land, and in sea and sky, are linked to a coastal area called Rohu. Rohu is connected with the activities of an army working "deep inside the island"; its soldiers are white men who work with *kakamora* in "a secret high-tech urban-military complex" underground (Scott, 2016: 484). The strange things people see around Makira are signs that the army and *kakamora* are at work on a plan to restore authentic Makiran language, custom, and authority. Scott does not reduce Arosi wonder discourse to a tidy and comforting logic of redemption. He points out that although Makirans believe the end times are coming because of the underground army's work, they remain baffled by how it will happen and what, exactly, to think about the strange sights they see. He notes that different Arosi come to different conclusions. One man, Hoanidangi, finds pleasure in refusing explanation. Confusion is "a positive experience" for him, "a state of mind to be welcomed and even talked up" (488). Discourse about wondrous things fosters interest in seeing new wonders and considering the mysterious activities they might indicate. The landscape of Rohu, with its seaside cliffs and crevices, is geologically remarkable; but the beings springing forth from it, according to Scott, are ultimately the product of Arosi ontological transformation as they grapple with the question of whether they are essentially divided or united in their attachments to each other and their land.

An example of a movement in which blood, death, and geography are all pulled into the complex work of sacred placemaking is Jim Jones's Peoples Temple. Jones's settlement in the jungles of Guyana, colloquially known as Jonestown, is often held up as an example of how badly wrong a new religion can go when a leader's charisma becomes absolutist and detached from his followers' welfare. In establishing Jonestown, Jones sought a "Promised Land" resonant with African American Christian beliefs. The promise of this new land was not just the opportunity to build a socialist paradise with racial equality, but also safety from the effects of nuclear war. Guyana appealed to Jones for its government's socialist agenda, its population's large demographic with African heritage, its use of the English language, and its remoteness from the destruction expected from an atomic Armageddon (Moore, 2009: see also Guinn, 2017).

When more than nine hundred people were killed or committed suicide at Jonestown on November 18, 1978, the Promised Land became a site of destruction and loss. The horrific event did not secure Jonestown's place as a sacred site, however – indeed, it arguably unraveled any claim to sacredness Jonestown might have had. The United States government wanted the bodies to be buried in Jonestown, but the Guyanese government – perhaps anticipating how bodies can enchant the graves in which they lay – refused, and the bodies were taken to Dover Air Force Base in Delaware for forensic identification (Moore, 2011: 45). The riotously luxuriant jungle in Guyana began reclaiming space on the ground almost immediately.

Grieving family members in the United States needed a place to mark their loss. Wherever that would be, it would not be Jonestown itself. Nor would it be Delaware, where people worried that the state "might become a magnet for other cults, or even serve as a shrine to Jonestown" (Moore, 2021: 191). Eventually, a cemetery in Oakland, California, agreed to hold the remains of around four hundred unidentified and unclaimed people. One reason Oakland made sense as a burial site was because of Peoples Temple's strong connections to the Bay Area. Another reason, however, was geographical affordance: African American funerary traditions discourage cremation, so where would four hundred coffins fit? Stacked, it turns out, within "an excavated hillside with a magnificent view of San Francisco Bay" (Moore, 2021: 192). To dedicate the ground as a memorial, a simple monument was erected in 1979. In 2011, a new memorial was created featuring four plaques set into the ground, inscribed with the names of all who died. The inclusion of Jim Jones's name enraged an African American church leader who felt that Jones's evil meant that his name should be excluded; she had been working for years on her own plans for a memorial (Moore, 2021: 193–203).

Paul Manning (2017: 67) writes persuasively that "landscapes act as a narrative affordance, something that does not determine, but affords – enables or constrains – the plausible telling of specific kinds of narratives with respect to specific kinds of landscapes." His claim resonates well with Ivy's discussion of Mount Osore, and he points to Dartmoor's tors as another place whose natural features encourage spectral imagination. Jonestown complicates the discussion of geography, because the site where people died was in a remote jungle and in a different country than where nearly all of the victims came from. In addition, the government in charge was keen to remove the people, the event, and its memories from their map.[4] The mourning site has become a cemetery in Oakland which was near Peoples Temple's base of support and also had enough space to inter hundreds of coffins – but, as we will discuss in Section 6, the most

---

[4] At the end of 2024, the government of Guyana announced plans for a private company to give commercial tours of Jonestown, a proposal met with wide opposition in Guyana, https://jonestown.sdsu.edu/?page_id=129289.

visited memorial to Jonestown is a website. Particular physical features can lend themselves to a place's sacred aura, but the work of making places sacred is never predetermined by landscape, and it is never finished, either. Humans continually need to do the performative work of sacralization.

4 Performing the Sacred

Any place, no matter what it looks like, can become sacred through people's actions. That is what this Element is about. But besides seeing extraordinary visions, shedding blood, building monuments, and marveling at weird geological forms, what else do people do to mark places as sacred, as linked to the extrahuman?

It might sound obvious, but we need to mention that people *speak* places into sacredness. That is, they declare particular places to be sacred, baptizing or consecrating them. These actions are performative in J. L. Austin's sense, meaning they effect what they express (Austin, 1975). For example, when a person says "I promise," they are doing what they say – they are promising, not just referring to promises in general. Performative speech both depends on and reinforces social expectations, and can create new identities. When a marriage celebrant says, "I now pronounce you husband and wife," the couple practically do become a husband and a wife to each other. Obviously, many conditions need to support the delivery of this performative speech: the couple need to have legally registered their marriage (itself another performative declaration, although usually written) and the celebrant needs to be licensed to speak those words, at a minimum. In her influential book *Gender Trouble*, Judith Butler (1990) expanded Austin's argument to describe how people become gendered subjects through performative acts, and performativity has proven to be a usefully expansive analytical term (see, e.g., Kulick, 2003).

Keith H. Basso worked with people in the community of Cibecue, on the Fort Apache Indian Reservation in Arizona, to understand how they speak a landscape into sacredness. It can be easy to imagine indigenous groups like Native Americans as somehow being more "in touch" with the natural world, but left as a presupposition this is simply a stereotype. Basso shows in detail how Apache speakers actively enchant the landscape by naming and narrating it. Place names can be geographical descriptions (such as T'iis Ts'ósé Bił Naagolgaiyé, "Circular Clearing with Slender Cottonwood Trees") or referents to events (such as 'Istaa Hadaanáyołé, "Widows Pause for Breath," where three sisters lamented their late husbands; Basso, 1996: 23, 28). Most place names are complete sentences, and they are often used in storytelling to anchor audiences' visual and moral imaginations. Many stories have moral lessons, and can be told to reprimand particular listeners. As Basso observes, "every historical tale is also 'about' the person at whom it is directed" (55).[5]

But place names, and the stories in which they are wrapped, do more than simply give moral instruction. They link ancestors, living people, and places so firmly as to unite their identities and senses of being. "For Indian men and women," Basso writes:

> the past lies embedded in features of the earth – in canyons and lakes, mountains and arroyos, rocks and vacant fields – which together endow their lands with multiple forms of significance that reach into their lives and shape the ways they think. Knowledge of places is therefore closely linked to knowledge of the self, to grasping one's position in the larger scheme of things, including one's own community, and to securing a confident sense of who one is as a person... [I]n acts of speech, mundane and otherwise, Apaches fashion images and understandings of the land that are accepted as credible accounts of what it actually is, why it is significant, and how it impinges on the daily lives of men and women. In short, portions of a world view are constructed and made available, and a Western Apache version of the landscape is deepened, amplified, and tacitly affirmed. With words, a massive physical presence is fashioned into a meaningful human universe. (1996: 34, 40)

Basso shows how an understanding of Apache wisdom does not require the assumption of inherent connections between the ancient past and sacredness, but, rather, focuses attention to the energetic and ongoing work people do to make places sacred – in this case, by speaking their names, elaborating their stories, and directing their judgments.

The work of speaking places into sacredness can take place institutionally. For example, in the United Methodist Church, the service for consecrating a church building includes the performative statement (spoken by whomever has been chosen to do so – it does not need to be a particular official) – "I [or "we"] present this building to be consecrated for the worship of God and the service of all people." A bishop or district superintendent formally asks, "By what name shall this house be known?" and a pastor or lay representative responds, "It shall be called the [Name] United Methodist Church." Then comes the announcement: "Dear friends, rejoice that God so moved the hearts of people that this house has been built for praise and prayer. Let us now consecrate it for service and celebrate its holy use." A prayer follows. The pulpit, baptismal

---

[5] Basso observes a difference between what he calls historical tales, which are short and delivered in plain language, and myths and sagas. "Whereas myths and sagas may take hours to complete, historical tales can usually be delivered in less than five minutes. Western Apache storytellers point out that this is both fitting and effective, because [historical] stories, like the arrows they are commonly said to represent, work best when they move swiftly" (1996: 51).

font, and communion table are also verbally consecrated as part of the complete service (Discipleship Ministries, 2013).

As the historian Andrew Spicer observes, Christian views on church buildings' sacredness evolve over time. Martin Luther did not think people needed churches in which to preach the Word of God, and Reformers stopped performing the medieval consecration rite (Spicer, 2006: 209). Indeed, while inaugurating a new chapel at Hartenfels Castle, Luther preached in a way seemingly contrary to the occasion, declaring that "If the occasion should arise that the people did not want to or could not assemble [there], one could just as well preach outside by the fountain" (209). In early seventeenth-century England, however, a countermovement gained momentum. Although churchmen like William Laud were keen not to be seen as "Popish" (a derogatory term for Catholics) by getting caught up in material displays, they insisted that church space really is different and needs to be recognized for its special divine purpose.[6] New liturgies were written, and new debates arose over the centrality of bishops to consecration (Spicer, 2006: 215–16). Thus, the question, "Are churches sacred sites?" which might seem to have an obvious answer, receives different responses at different times.

Ostensibly secular institutions can gain an aura of sacredness when they represent intangible heritage and national traditions. For example, this occurs when previously religious objects are relocated to museums and heritage sites, or when religion-themed paintings are placed in art galleries for public display (Ryde, 2009; Brown, 2016). As modern secular institutions emerging from the Enlightenment, museums and galleries mostly focus on aesthetics and historical context for educational, entertainment, and tourism purposes (Duncan, 1995; Minucciani, 2013; Mairesse, 2019). To fulfill these purposes, objects and artworks are sometimes placed behind glass windows, displayed to the public, and reinterpreted as cultural relics (Willis, 2015; Zhu, 2018). Michael Ames (1992: 23) uses the term "museumification" to describe such processes in the display of sacred objects, which result in "sanitising, insulating, plasticising, and preserving them as attractions and simple lesson aids." Religious objects can be displaced and disassociated from their original contexts, taking on new meanings of historical or aesthetic authenticity through the eyes of historians, archaeologists, or museologists (Grimes, 1992). For modern secularized nation-states, the reinterpretation of religious objects imbues them with historical value, connecting them to emblematic local customs and traditions, thus

---

[6] As one author wrote in 1642, "Christs voyce is more heard and his graces more seene in the Word and Sacraments within our Churches then anywhere else. Where should the King be more seene and heard then in his owne house? It is his house by inhabitation, for though all our houses be his because the earth is the Lords, and all that therein is, yet this house is more specially his … here he dwels more particularly" (Spicer, 2006: 207–8, original spelling retained).

building and representing national culture (Kong, 2005; Nyíri, 2006; Kang, 2009; Preziosi, 2014; Pimenova, 2022).

A glass cabinet in a museum can encourage, rather than prevent, individuals from interpreting the object inside as sacred (Paine, 2013; Berns, 2016). Once objects are frozen in time to "preserve" their original authenticity, museums and heritage sites can create different forms of spiritual power or generate an "aura" in Walter Benjamin's (2008) sense. As discussed above, the idea of sacredness is not universal but rather grounded in people's lived experiences and daily practices, the human interactions that (re)activate meaning, and the moments and spaces in which such practices unfold (Zhu, Wang, and Rowlands, 2020). In this context, a new form of sacred aura is generated through people's engagement with objects in museums and heritage sites (Macdonald, 2005; Brulon Soares, 2019).

For instance, Yujie has observed many occasions when Buddhist laypeople still kneel and pray to Buddhist relics, now treated as antique objects within museum windows in China. For them, the glass window and modern interpretation and rebranding of religious objects as antiques are merely representations that do not change their personal association with those objects and spaces. What holds significant sacred value for these religious practitioners are various acts of "doing," such as bowing, kneeling, and praying (Chau, 2011). It is through these actions that they create personal relationships that generate religious meaning and efficacy (Macdonald, 2005; Wallis, 2012; Paine, 2013). A similar phenomenon has been observed by Neil MacGregor, the director of the National Gallery in London, when he saw individuals praying to religious paintings or artifacts (Brown, 2016: 131).

While the idea of the sacred is often associated with separation from the secular world in Western contexts, concepts of sacred and secular often intertwine in multifunctional practices (Asad, 1999, 2003; della Dora, 2018; Fleeson, 2023). In historical China, where Buddhism, Daoism, and folk religion were often associated with mountains and natural landscapes, individuals travelled to these sites as both sacred and secular spaces (Nyíri, 2006; Zhu and Li, 2013). They visited them to seek blessings, eat vegetarian food, and engage in self-cultivation and leisure with friends. In the modern context, when these mountains and natural landscapes have been transformed into national heritage parks and scenic sites, the spatial transformations of modern logic do not entirely disentangle sacred and secular (Oakes, 1998; Nyíri, 2006; Zhu and Li, 2013).[7]

---

[7] This multifunctionality and diversity of space are similar to what was revealed by Dafydd Jones's (2019) study of Muslim worship in Wales. Mosques are places for people to worship and study Islamic teachings, but also serve as community centers simply to communicate, to socialize, to relax, and to exchange information.

Modern nation-states create new kinds of sacred sites distinct from traditional religious sites such as temples, churches, and cathedrals. One significant example is the establishment of war memorials around the world, particularly following the memory boom after the First and Second World Wars (Winter, 2006; Macdonald, 2013). Although the infrastructure of war memorials differs from that of most modern heritage sites and museums holding religious objects, they often create senses of sacredness through architecture and the display of statues meant to convey a sense of monumentality and eternity (Viejo-Rose, 2011). For instance, the Australian War Memorial in Canberra is constructed similarly to a mausoleum (see Figure 5). The central "Commemorative Courtyard" is edged with a necrology of the 103,000 Australians killed in wars since 1885. The Hall of Memory above the Pool of Reflection contains the Tomb of the Unknown Australian Soldier. The design creates a sacred space for people to commemorate the dead.

Senses of sacredness can also be cultivated through personalized rituals (Macdonald, 2005, 2013; Teeger and Vinitzky-Seroussi, 2007; Zwigenberg, 2014). For instance, the Nagasaki Atomic Bomb Museum serves as a remembrance of the atomic bombing of the Japanese city by the United States (see Figure 6). In addition to displaying historical interpretations to help the public understand the horrors of war and nuclear weapons and the importance of peace, the museum has also designed a memorial hall for the public to meditate and reflect in silence. While such practices are not associated with any religion, it is through acts of prayer and reflection that the space becomes connected to sacred moments of contemplation.

War memorials, like distinct religious objects, can be used for nation-building purposes (Macdonald, 2013; 2015; Berger and Tekin, 2018; Nakano and Zhu, 2020). This is seen at the Nanjing Massacre Memorial in China (see Figure 7), where commemorative ceremonies foster a *lieu de mémoire* (site of memory) for the populace to engage in a specific form of national memory (Qian, 2009; Violi, 2012; Denton, 2014; Zhu, 2022). In this way, the sacred becomes a political tool for identity-building in a secular society, while religious practice and modern techniques of nation-building becoming notably hard to distinguish.

Buildings established as secular places can become sacred over time, in whole or part. We don't just mean ruins, whose mute attestation to past lives can evoke a sense of connection with the dead. We mean newly sanctified spaces, like chapels within airports (Cadge, 2018). In the United States, Catholics began establishing sacred spaces within airports in the early 1950s; in 1970, Pope Paul VI caught up with the trend and formed a commission "to study and provide pastoral care to people on the move including air travelers" (Cadge, 2018: 141). In the 1970s and 1980s, a multifaith "Protestant–Catholic–Jewish model" for

Figure 5 Australian War Memorial courtyard, January 10, 2023. Photo by Matt Tomlinson.

sacred spaces developed, with many airports providing a single room for different groups to share. Since the 1990s, Wendy Cadge notes, more markedly Muslim spaces have been established in airports even as the Protestant–Catholic–Jewish model has been transformed in some places into generic "meditation rooms" and "reflection rooms."

The establishment of Muslim prayer rooms was something Matt observed at his workplace, the H. C. Coombs Building at the Australian National University in Canberra. The Coombs Building's cornerstone was laid in 1961. One of the original

Figure 6 The Nagasaki Atomic Bomb Museum, September 2019. Photo by Yujie Zhu.

designs for the Coombs "called for a series of separate pavilions and courts symmetrically arranged around a central water feature, a moat bordering an island with a 'Tea House of the August Moon': a kind of summer palace, as one observer remarked, with a distinctive tropical ambiance" (Lal, 2014: 12). The design was not sacred, but it was undeniably "both grandiose and impractical," and a competing bid won (13–14). The winning design was its own whimsical creature, described by one author as "like a very complex system of wombat burrows arranged to give the wombats stimulating intellectual challenges in finding their way about" (Warden, 2013). A trio of interlocking hexagons, the quirky building has inspired a book of creative scholarly reflections on the space and its community (Lal and Ley, 2014). More to the point, now decades into its existence, it has begun hosting serious acts of sacred placemaking. When the Coombs was refurbished late in the 2010s, Islamic prayer rooms were added at the urging of some groups that had been part of the consultation process, as well as the college's dean at the time.

Paul Girrawah House, a Ngambri-Kamberri, Walgalu, Wiradyuri, and Ngunnawal custodian, artist, and officer in the Australian National University's First Nations Portfolio, was born at the heart of his ancestral lands, at the old Canberra hospital, Ngambri (Kamberri) Country. In late 2023, House began carving traditional/contemporary designs into native trees surrounding the

Making Places Sacred 25

Figure 7 Peace Square, Memorial Hall, Nanjing Massacre Memorial, China, November 2019. Photo by Yujie Zhu.

Coombs Building in order to mark it publicly as Aboriginal territory – in particular "to reclaim Country, one tree at a time," reclaiming Country that was never given up by his Old People, rather land that was stolen by colonizers without consent or treaty (see Figure 8). Considering the site's deep history, as well as the Aboriginal cultural objects, material and human ancestors stored inside the building, House was moved to begin tree-carving on-site to ritually define it as both Aboriginal land and inviolably sacred, acknowledging, respecting and honoring his Ngambri-Kamberri ancestors and Country.

The story of the Coombs Building becoming a more markedly sacred space through time with the addition of prayer rooms and creation of tree carvings might surprise readers, because university buildings do not seem like prime candidates for projects of sacralization. True, some buildings might be known for their sheer age or beautiful architecture, or memories of influential student protests or the ghosts of long-dead residents. What strikes us as notable about the Coombs is the presence of multiple forms of sacredness within an ostensibly secular space. And we have not even mentioned the Buddha there.[8]

---

[8] The wooden Buddha figure, made by a Cambodian artist and an Australian student, does not seem to be used much for worship, but it has inspired an academic reflection on the material collection inside the Coombs Building (Fox, 2014).

Figure 8 Tree carving by Paul Girrawah House, H. C. Coombs Building, Australian National University, November 9, 2023. Photo by Matt Tomlinson.

Coopting another group's sacred site to make it one's own sacred site is a practice with a deep and expansive history. For example, in Damascus, a temple dedicated to Jupiter was replaced by a Christian basilica, which was in turn knocked down to be the site of the Umayyad Mosque (Emmett, 2009: 453). An especially well-known example is the Hagia Sophia in Istanbul. It lasted nearly a millennium as a Christian church until Sultan Mehmet II transformed it into a mosque in 1453; it remained a Muslim site for almost 500 years until 1934, when it became a secular museum; then in 2020 the president of Turkey, Recep Tayyip Erdoğan, declared it to be a functioning mosque again (Croke, 2022). Appropriations can be peaceful, too – "throughout the United States there are many instances where churches have been sold to Muslim congregations for use as mosques" – and spaces can be shared, even by supposedly competing groups: Muslims are welcome to pray in the south apse of Bethlehem's Church of the Nativity because Caliph 'Umar once did so, and church officials have removed "religious images from the south apse so as not to offend the Muslims who came to pray" (Emmett, 2009: 458, 461).

New Religious Movements can coopt established sacred sites or develop their own. To return to the example of Spiritualism, many Spiritualist congregations rent space for their meetings – although those who manage to obtain their own premises gain institutional durability (Singleton and Tomlinson, 2025). For those who rent, even the plainest multipurpose room in a community center becomes a sacred site when people gather there to connect with extrahuman figures and forces. However, in Spiritualism and some other NRMs, bodies, rather than buildings, are the key sacred sites. They are also the ones most vulnerable.

5 The Body – the Most Vulnerable Sacred Site

It is natural to think of our bodies as the grounds of experience. We engage with the world sensually, and attempts to escape or supersede our bodies – for example in shamanism, dream travel, or other out-of-body experiences – end in a return to the physical. Yet as Marcel Mauss pointed out in "The Notion of Body Techniques" (1979), the ways we hold, move, and bend our bodies vary widely by cultural training. Things that seem as natural as walking, sitting, and falling asleep are given different shapes by bodies trained in different ways. It makes sense, then, that there is no single way in which people use their bodies to connect with sacredness or become sacred in themselves. Moreover, because our bodies eventually age, weaken, and return to earth in some form, they afford an especially vulnerable kind of cultivation of the sacred.

Prosperity Christianity's hallmark is its emphasis on growth and abundance, an emphasis so strong that it can sound like Max Weber's Protestant Ethic on steroids: If you truly believe in God, the Holy Spirit will infuse your body with blessings, allowing you to cast out demons, improve your heath, and gain wealth. Simon Coleman (2000: 127–8), working with such a congregation in Sweden, describes their understanding of scripture and speech's tangible power: the Bible is consumable, the Word of God needs to be devoured. The metaphor recurs as people speak of being hungry for it, being filled with it, or, as one pastor said, "like a Sumo wrestler, you become the biggest when you eat God's Word." Being filled with God's word means one can deploy it. For example, a woman battling hay fever explains that she "shot" biblical words into her room – "I went around the room and peppered Satan" (132).

Coleman observes how this church's expectations of how language works shape adherents' understandings of their bodies and the spaces they inhabit, uniting them in sacred purpose. He describes how at services in Uppsala and London, he and thousands of other audience members were

> urged to turn collectively to the four points of the compass and to claim, in the name of God, the unsaved cultural territories stretching out before us. Rather than stretching out to a sacred, distant centre, as would be the case in a genuflection towards Mecca, the congregation is encouraged here to think of themselves, wherever they happen to be, as the spiritual centre of action. (Coleman, 2000: 136)

This philosophy of language, in which sacred words accrete inside sacralized bodies that then bless the world, might seem to make believers almost invulnerable – but of course they suffer the ravages of time, injury, and disease as anyone else does. Suffering causes significant distress not only due to pain, but also due to the failure of ideology seen in the inability to speak good health into existence. One Bible School student left her study course because she could not harmonize the church's "triumphalist" message with her own failing health (138).

Spiritualist mediums face the same challenge of reconciling their experiences of physical pain and weakness with a stout belief in the body's ability to receive spiritual healing. A common assertion in Spiritualism is that "There is no such thing as death," meaning that when one dies physically, one keeps living at a more refined level of energy. One is promoted to the astral plane. This does not mean that Spiritualists do not get upset when loved ones die, or that they are looking forward to their own physical demise. They don't like death any more than Sufis, Quakers, or Baha'i do. But they insist that one can cultivate good health through positive thinking, and can share healing energy with other people, either through mental and spiritual projection or by laying hands on them. A famous British spirit healer named Harry Edwards described spirit healing as "a thought process," and an influential spirit guide named Silver Birch, who spoke through another British medium named Maurice Barbanell, declared: "The more you think of perfect health, the closer you come towards attaining it" (Edwards and Branch, 1974: 17; Storm, 1969: 131).[9]

Spiritualists distinguish between "physical mediumship" and "mental mediumship," and in both practices mediums make themselves vulnerable by

---

[9] Spiritualists are hardly the only religious group to insist on the power of positive thinking and to say that death, as commonly understood, does not exist. Coleman (2000: 138n21) describes how in the Swedish Pentecostal church he studied, "funerals do not take a prominent role in ... literature or other forms of public discourse. Occasionally, I have heard stories of believers being unable to accept the death of younger members of the group, and even suggesting that a Lazarus-like resurrection might be possible."

using their bodies as instruments for connecting with spirit beings. Physical mediumship involves the production of tangible evidence of otherworldly presence, most famously in the form of "ectoplasm" – oozy matter emerging from mediums' bodies, sometimes taking the shape of the spirit beings attempting to "come through." The production of ectoplasm is thought to require a great deal of energy which can cause damage if not properly managed. The British medium Doris Stokes tells an illustrative story about a famous physical medium, Gordon Higginson, who had an accident when both of them were at the Arthur Findlay College. Stokes was recovering from the flu and did not attend a séance Higginson was holding, but sensed that something had happened to him. Alarmed, she raced out of her room and saw a group of men carrying Higginson, who seemed to have been badly injured. "We never did find out exactly what had happened," Stokes recalls, "but apparently Gordon had forgotten he was wearing a metal buckle on his belt. There had been some disturbance during the seance which had caused the ectoplasm to return to Gordon's body with such force, his metal buckle had become red hot and burned him. . . . The skin round the navel was angry red and bubbling with blisters" (Stokes and Dearsley, 1981: 124–5).

In Spiritualism, mental mediumship is theoretically safer than physical mediumship because it simply involves mediums' receiving signs of spirit presence in their minds and bodies, not manifesting them outwardly. One type of sign they can receive, however, is the sensation of how a person died. Although such experiences are not considered dangerous, they can be disturbing, and show the medium's bodily vulnerability. A Spiritualist medium in Canberra named Jane Hall told Matt:

> If someone [has had] a heart attack, I'll feel pressure on my chest. And when you're developing [as a medium], that's quite a frightening feeling. Because it's like – *whoa, is this me? Am I having a heart attack? Or am I – what's going on?* And then you just ask [people in the spirit world] to take [the feeling] away, and they take it away as quick as that. . . . I will know if somebody's had a brain aneurysm. . . . I'll start to feel it in my head. My head will start to feel a pressure. . . . I will know when there is medication on board. So if somebody has had opioids because they are in the end of cancer, I will feel that. Because I'll just start to feel myself being kind of groggy. And I can just feel being dizzy. . . . Things like transfusions, blood transfusions. . . . It's a very different feeling because you'll feel your blood vessels. You'll feel . . . a rush in your arm. . . . It's very clear when somebody's taken their life with a – if they've [hanged] themselves, you'll feel very much – you can feel that. Having said that, a lot of people don't like to show you that, when they've taken their own life. But yeah, you can physically feel these things.

Although the main purpose of Spiritualist mediums' work is to bring love and reassurance to people that their late family and friends still exist, the insistence on evidence – *prove to me that you are really in touch with the spirit of my grandmother* – means mediums train themselves to sacralize their own bodies as sites of spiritual communication, and this sacralization makes mediums vulnerable to the distressing pain felt by the sick and dying.

In some cultural contexts, rather than concentrate sacredness in one's own body, one projects it onto other bodies that are seen as radically different. In his analysis of tourists' encounters with Korowai people of Papua (eastern Indonesia), Rupert Stasch describes how for tourists from places like Europe and the United States, Korowai seem to embody the perfect primitive life. They live in the jungle, hunt for food, and live in houses on stilts that reach into the tree canopy. Their seemingly carefree life makes sense to tourists through comparison to pop culture examples; for example, Korowai are compared to the Ewoks from Star Wars. Visiting Korowai is not just a cheap thrill, however. Indeed, Stasch argues that for tourists, "the encounters are rituals of direct sensory experience of exoticizing stereotypes that partake of qualities of the transcendent or sacred" (Stasch, 2016: 11). In a way, Korowai come to seem godlike to tourists: they are seen as primitive, which implies that they are inherently spiritual and in ecological harmony with their environment. But by "agitating" tourists' self-understandings – that is, making tourists reflect on their own lives and values – Korowai also come to seem in part like monsters to their visitors. They might be cannibals, or violent, or unreliable in disturbing ways (15).

Korowai also see tourists as extrahuman, and also not in an entirely good way. Tourists are compared to demons and invisible gods who live in tabooed places. This explains why tourists are so odd, and rich, and sometimes angry. But this characterization of tourists does not lead Korowai to shun their visitors. Instead, Korowai want to enter into exchange relations with them. Korowai do not covet the food tourists bring, the cameras they point, or the backpacks they carry, but realize that developing material exchange relations with them will help Korowai sort out their own local problems. For example, they need money for their children's schooling, and they have fights with each other over bride-taking and pig-killing which demand compensation. Having access to tourists' wealth would mean they could better achieve their own ideals of what Korowai society should be like. As the anthropologist Marshall Sahlins (1992: 13) wrote of Pacific Islanders' understandings of development, for Korowai, tourism agitates the idea that they might be able to achieve "their own culture on a bigger and better scale than they ever had it."[10]

---

[10] Stasch refers to a striking photo in which a small-statured Korowai man, clad only in a loincloth, with his buttocks exposed, shakes hands with a Swiss filmmaker wearing shorts and a T-shirt and carrying a camping backpack. The Korowai man is at the left of the photo and the filmmaker is on

Another anthropologist, Aparecida Vilaça, describes an indigenous group in Brazil who believe their own bodies to be inherently capable of transforming between modes of existence. Whereas Korowai and tourists interact to some extent at arm's length – they are always accompanied by tour guides who know the territory – the Wari' people of the Amazon keep identity and otherness within themselves as always coexistent possibilities.

For the Wari', to be human means to be a predator. Humans consume; animals are consumed (Vilaça, 2005, 2016). In a gendered extension of this principle, men sexually "consume" women, although this does not mean women are associated with animals in a way men are not, because the key issue in Wari' ontology is that all bodies are fundamentally unstable due to the creative power of perspective. A human sees a jaguar as an animal, something to kill. But that jaguar, being a predator, sees itself as human, and sees humans as jaguars to be hunted. Moreover, beings can unintentionally transform between species. A human who sees other humans and socializes with them, not realizing that they are really jaguars, becomes a jaguar due to being near them and eating the same food as them. Upon returning to her kin, this person is recognized as substantially and dangerously different. If your kin are eating worms and claiming their meal is meat, or sleeping in trees and declaring that they are really in hammocks, you know they are truly other than what they seem (2005: 454).

Wari' worry about human instability and try to secure their humanity through various means. A person nurtures and cares for kin, ensuring through commensality that they will really be human, just like you are (or so you believe). Another is to consult shamans, who have the ability to see what species other beings "really" are. Another means presented itself when Christian missionaries brought the Bible, which says that humans were divinely created separately from animals and other beings (Genesis 1). Wari' were glad to receive this message (Vilaça, 2016: 132–5). They were concerned, however, by Christian teachings about hell, which indicated that non-Christians will be roasted eternally without their bodies being consumed, making them "prey forever" (138). Wari' funerary practice requires affines (relatives by marriage) of the deceased to consume parts of the body in order to compel the bereaved consanguines (blood relatives) to see that this person is now dead and consumed (2005:

---

the right side. Stasch writes: "The tourist on the right ... feels he wants to *become* the person on the left, whom he admires as a quasi divinity because of his total lack of manufactured consumer goods. Meanwhile, the person on the left feels he wants to *become* the person on the right, whom he admires as a quasi divinity because of his unlimited access to manufactured consumer goods" (2016: 8; emphases in original). In short, Korowai and tourists envy and exalt each other, turning their partners into extrahuman figures, but they also denigrate each other. Primitivity is not entirely virtuous for tourists, and Korowai resent tourists' failure to participate in truly beneficial exchange.

454–5). If hellfire does not finish the work of consumption, then Christian theology seems to reaffirm humanity's existential instability after having solved it with the account of divine creation in the first chapter of Genesis.

Bodies seem like natural sites of sacralization, but, as with the other sites and dynamics we have discussed so far, the means vary almost endlessly. Penitents whipping themselves to erase their sins connect sacredness with the body in a very different way than Spiritualist mediums do, and Pentecostals who depict Christ as a muscleman have a starkly different imagination of the sacred than Catholics who focus on the vulnerable, wounded Christ on the cross (e.g., Cannell, 1999). Our point here is simply that bodies are especially vulnerable material. Whether people deny this vulnerability and seek visions of eternal life, or embrace it and devoutly shape their bodies to be temples, the sacredness of bodies is always a fragile and temporary thing.

6 Sacred Space Is Multidimensional

It seems almost too obvious to mention that places exist in relation to elsewheres – to other, different places. But the point should nonetheless be stated explicitly, if only to ground ourselves for a consideration of the many dimensions in which sacred spaces are imagined and made.

Mircea Eliade's analysis of the *axis mundi*, a "universal pillar" connecting the earth with the heavens above and the underworld below, and which serves as "the very center of the universe," is one model of how sacred spaces can be configured (1961: 36–7). A different model is the regional system of sacred sites and local ritual expertise developed by the Mountain Ok peoples of Papua New Guinea (Robbins, 2004: chapter 2). Joel Robbins writes that within this system, the Urapmin people were custodians of a cave called Wim Tem and were the ones to perform rituals within it. Rather than analyze the cave à la Eliade as a chthonic connection of below with above, Robbins observes that the site was sacred because it was part of a network across territories. Different Mountain Ok lands, with different owners holding site-specific secret knowledge and ritual expertise, worked together for the greater good. By working at Wim Tem, Urapmin helped ensure the prosperity of all Mountain Ok; other groups likewise did their part, maintaining locally distinctive knowledge and ritual practices in order to benefit people throughout the region.[11]

Pilgrimages, as journeys to or among sacred sites, model sacred space's multidimensionality. Examples include movement from far-flung lands to

---

[11] We are phrasing this summary in the past tense because of Robbins' focus on how Urapmin became Christians and the practical, moral, and intellectual challenges entailed by their conversion. He observes that the disruptions of colonialism and arrival of Christianity created a new

sacred centers, like Mecca; others are "oriented toward pathways rather than centers," as Simon Coleman (2022: 217) observes. He adds that pilgrimages along pathways foster "generalized spiritualities rather than overt religiosities, and forms of slow movement articulated in opposition to, and yet interlinked with, experiences of hypermobility."

A good example of this kind of pathway pilgrimage is Japan's Shikoku Henro, a circuit of 88 temples (Hayes, 2021: 198–9; see also Reader, 2005). The spirituality that Shikoku pilgrims cultivate is associated in part with hardship and death, as the complete journey takes longer than a month to complete if one walks the entire route; some parts of the path are arduous; and the pilgrimage was traditionally undertaken by people who sought healing from illness. Because a pilgrim's outfit is white, and white symbolizes death in Japan, the original permit granted to pilgrims stated that "There is no need to contact the bearer's home village in case she [or he] drops dead of illness. Please have mercy and bury this person after death" (Hayes, 2021: 202; brackets in original). In addition, the most common reason given for taking the pilgrimage, according to a 2011 survey, is to honor a deceased loved one. Carol Hayes points out that pilgrims are surrounded by signs urging them onward, including many statues of the Buddhist monk who established the path, Kōbō Daishi, as well as many texts including pilgrims' notebooks which temple monks stamp and date; phrases of encouragement written on pilgrims' bags and hats; and anonymous poems people scatter on signs along the pathway for those who follow them.

To return to sacred centers, it bears mention that even the most seemingly fixed sacred site is woven into a temporal scheme in which attention to sacredness can wax and wane. Although making a pilgrimage to Mecca is considered spiritually worthy at any time for Muslims, doing it during the Hajj season is obligatory, a pillar of Islam. The round-island circuit made by the figure and priests of Lono during the Hawaiian new year period made the land fruitful and also arguably set the conditions for the killing of Captain Cook (Sahlins, 1985, 1995; compare Obeyesekere, 1992 and Sissons, 2014).

The matter of sacred space's temporality is given dazzling ethnographic treatment in Tom Boylston's ethnography *The Stranger at the Feast* (2018). Responding to anthropological work that examines how Christians seek material signs of God's presence, Boylston writes that in northern Ethiopia's Zege Peninsula, God is considered so overwhelmingly present that people must draw boundaries around the sacred. The challenge for Orthodox Christians on the Zege Peninsula is not finding signs of divine presence but keeping them

---

regional order that made Urapmin "remote" in a way they had never been before. One of their motivations to convert to Christianity was to become part of a ritual network again.

manageable. A fourteenth-century Orthodox monk was divinely guided to the peninsula, and told followers that the land was to be marked as sacred by using only their hands to farm, and by prohibiting plowing and tree-cutting. The entire peninsula is thus considered sacred land, and the forest of coffee trees that grows on it is considered especially sacred. Within those forests, churches and monasteries have a heightened sacredness. Within those sites are several ever-more-sacred interior spaces: "The Eucharist is prepared in the inner sanctum of a church, surrounded by multiple concentric walls, each marking an increase in the purity and observance required to enter" (Boylston, 2018: 56).

This model of ever-concentrated inner sacredness is temporally cross-cut by the ritual calendar. No matter when the coffee ripens, it must be harvested only after the Feast of the Epiphany, observed on the nineteenth of January. Manual labor is forbidden on saints' days. And fasting is a key ritual practice, one practiced with a frequency that would astonish followers of less demanding traditions. Boylston reports that

> everybody wanted to know if I kept the fast – primarily taking no meat on Wednesdays or Fridays or during Lent, but also potentially on a number of other occasions throughout the Christian calendar, amounting, if you were really strict, to more than 250 days of the year spent in either partial or total abstinence from food and drink. (2018: 42)

Although sacredness is typically time-bound in many traditions, for Ethiopian Orthodox Christians on the Zege peninsula, the rhythms of sanctification are as intense as the landscape's concentration of it.

Another kind of sacred space is the invisible world which people ritually gesture toward and invoke. Traditional ritual practitioners in the central Pacific nation of Kiribati do their work on atolls' ocean-facing sides, rather than their lagoons, because of the sea's association with spiritual power (Kempf, 2019: 130). Much of their ritual work is keyed to song and dance composition and performance. The source of their ritual effectiveness inheres in the space between the shore and the horizon, wherein exists an invisible network of sites defined by ancestral action and presence. Some of the sites are said to be underwater; others are connected to sea or land features like waves and cliffs. Although the term "liminal" is overused in ritual studies, here it applies well: the spirits live in a space "between visibility and invisibility, real and imagined, near and distant, sound and silence" (120). To understand sacred space in traditional I-Kiribati terms, then, one must trace articulations among the ritual work done on shore with the invisible world of networked sites stretching from the space here – this sand, this surf – to the limits of perception at the horizon. "To set foot into this world is clearly not possible," Wolfgang Kempf observes, but its sacredness, manifest in music and dance, is ultimately accessible (2019: 132; see also Teaiwa, 2015).

The invisible network in Kiribati points to another dimension of sacred space: the virtual. Sacred space extends beyond physical locations into virtual environments (O'Leary, 1996; Inoue, 2000; Kong, 2001; Dawson and Cowan, 2004; Jacobs, 2007; Wagner, 2012). Many religious institutions worldwide have developed virtual spaces, allowing individuals to engage in digital worship and cyber-pilgrimages, and to cultivate personal relationships with sacred sites without needing to be physically present (Schroeder, Heather, and Lee, 1998; Hill-Smith, 2011; Campbell, 2013). O'Leary (1996) examines the implications of shifts in communication technology on religious discourse. Despite rapid technological advancements and the emergence of virtual mediators in the past three decades, O'Leary's points remain relevant. He posits that the traditional notion of the ritualistic power of symbolic action persists, although it is now confined to a limited domain within physical religious spaces and has found a new home in cyberspace. To illustrate this, he provides examples of worship conducted in electronic conference rooms on CompuServe (O'Leary, 1996).

For online rituals, virtual spaces can replicate the ambiance of traditional sacred environments through the use of sounds and sophisticated sensory designs, thereby facilitating transcendental experiences without the necessity of physical attendance. Similar to modern secular institutions such as museums, religious institutions simulate various sacred elements. Sounds and visual forms become particularly important in these virtual spaces, especially when certain senses such as touch and smell are disadvantaged. Connelly (2013) illustrated this in his analysis of silent Buddhist meditation within the virtual game Second Life. His study showed that participants felt they achieved spiritual merits through sight, sound, and touch with virtual artifacts such as the Buddha statue, the singing bowl, and the gong. This effectiveness is contingent on the ritual actions being performed with a unifying intention despite the absence of the physical senses of touch, smell, or taste.

In other instances, these sacred spaces are not replicas of existing sites but entirely new creations or supposed reconstructions of nonexistent spaces. Often, these virtual sacred spaces are constructed in virtual games for specific reasons (Wagner, 2012). For example, El Antably (2011) examines the virtual construction and reconstruction of the ancient South Asian city, Sirkap, in massively multiplayer online role-playing games. Nodes in these games are hubs of activity, existing as concentrations of buildings, artifacts, nonplayer characters, or interactive objects, such as the stupa court in Virtual Sirkap. A sense of sacredness is interactively created by a digital community when they gather online, follow orders of practice at virtual locales such as temples, mountains, or stones, and engage with each other through exchange, celebration, and other ritualized forms. Video games can be considered forms of sacred space which share features of order-making with other kinds of ritual performance (Wagner, 2014).

Virtual sacred space and place-making can affect real-world practices, including visits to physical sites (Wagner, 2014; Obadia, 2015; Jang, 2020). Production of virtual sacred spaces also influences the place-making of (often unofficial) real-world sites by digital communities (Yamamura, 2014; MacWilliams, 2023). This phenomenon is particularly evident in Japan's context of content tourism (Yamamura and Seaton, 2020), where enthusiasts of popular culture – such as movies, novels, games, and anime – organize *Seichi Junrei*, or pilgrimages to sacred spaces at real-world locations depicted in these media forms. Okamoto (2014) explores visits to anime-related sacred sites primarily by male fans of the otaku subculture. Through self-organized gatherings and rituals, these select locations are transformed into sites of worship and discussion around deities and sacred objects from anime, media, and games.

In Section 3, we observed how the work of making Jonestown sacred was multidimensional. Jim Jones sought a Promised Land, and his followers established their utopia in Guyana. The killing of Peoples Temple members in 1978 did not sanctify the land on which they had settled – quite the opposite happened, as the bodies were removed and jungle quickly reclaimed the site. A cemetery in Oakland became the resting place for four hundred victims and several monuments. The most effective memorial to Jonestown, however, is possibly the website "Alternative Considerations of Jonestown and Peoples Temple," established in 1998. It was created "to humanize the dead by remembering their lives and not only their deaths," and has become a notably active space of mourning, memory, and documentation (Moore, 2021: 195; see also Moore, 2011: 51–3). A popular section of the site, "Who Died," features stories and images about the victims, and over the years has come to attract comments from people who did not know them but nevertheless wish to pay tribute (Moore, 2011: 51–3).

The multidimensional interaction between virtual and physical spaces is a dynamic process, and studying it contributes significantly to our understanding of sacred space. This relationship reveals the evolving nature of sacred space in contemporary society, showing the diverse ways in which individuals seek and create meaning linked to extrahumanity in both virtual and real-world environments. And, as Connelly's discussion of Buddhist meditation in Second Life suggests, sacred space's multidimensionality invites consideration of its multisensory potential.

7 Sacred Space Is Multisensory

Touring the rural Fijian island of Kadavu in 1960, the anthropologist Rusiate Nayacakalou visited Tavuki, noting that it "bore the true marks of a chiefly village" (1975: 61). For one thing, leading representatives of the three main branches of Fijian authority lived there: the hereditary paramount chief (the Tui Tavuki), the government-appointed chief (the Roko Tui Kadavu), and the Methodist Church's district minister. For another, the enormous houses stood on giant earthen platforms, their sizes serving as signs of nobility. But perhaps the most impressive mark of Tavuki's chiefliness – and chiefliness is a deeply sacred category in indigenous Fiji – was its silence:

> The first impression I had was of a disturbing silence, but it was a reflection of the awe and respect with which the chiefs were held, not only by lower-ranking men but also by themselves in their relations with one another. There seemed to be a standing rule that children should not cry and cocks should not crow. The babbling of women beside houses working under the shade of trees, the laughter of young men preparing to go to the bush or to the sea, which often characterize village life in Fiji, were not at all common in Tavuki. Here the chiefs' houses dominated the village scene, and lesser men were bound by rules of respect towards chiefs to maintain silence in their presence. (Nayacakalou, 1975: 61–2)

The general hush over Tavuki indicated its chiefly status, reflecting the indigenous Fijian principle that chiefliness is expressed quietly (Arno, 1990; Nabobo-Baba, 2006). The silence and stillness embody a deep connection to the land, seen both as an inheritance from revered ancestors and as a divine gift from Jehovah (Tomlinson, 2009).

Although it would be simplistic to reduce Fijian sacredness to the silence manifest in its presence, it would be a mistake to overlook, or refuse to hear, the ways soundscapes can be integral to understandings of sacred space. Kaluli people of highland Papua New Guinea perceive spiritual presence primarily through sound. Indeed, living in a dense tropical forest, Kaluli consider sound to be more reliable than sight for knowing what is happening around them (Feld, 1982, 1996; Schieffelin, 1985). "The calls and voices of birds are especially prominent," Edward Schieffelin writes, "giving even an outsider the sense of hidden conversations. . . . Many kinds of bird calls are also the voices of spirit people" (1985: 710). Kaluli hold nighttime séances in longhouses at which entranced mediums sing songs for various purposes: to cure sick people; to find lost pigs; or simply to converse with spirits. Key to the songs' emotional force is the way they poetically name and connect places in the landscape, suggesting pathways which can be clues to listeners as to which spirit is speaking.

The sonic qualities of mediums' voices also shape people's understandings of who the spirits are and how they mean to engage with their listeners. In general, spirits' voices are "rather pinched and smaller than the medium's normal voice," but when the friendly spirit Kidel shows up, he expresses himself in a "deep friendly voice" and asks for tobacco (Schieffelin, 1985: 715). A young, unmarried female spirit uses "a coy falsetto voice" to flirt with young men; a small spirit man with a gigantic penis has "a squeaky voice and ... a shrill high-pitched laugh" and demands "to be given a woman"; dangerous spirits smack their lips and speak "in deep spooky voices," sometimes causing listeners to flee the longhouse in terror (716).

If a particular sound signifies something sacred, then its expression anywhere might seem to mark that place as sacred, too. Yet a more productive way to think about the relationship can be to consider the sound itself the sacred site. When Hare Krishnas chant the mantra "Hare Krishna, Hare Krishna, Krishna Krishna, Hare Hare, Hare Rama, Hare Rama, Rama Rama, Hare Hare," they believe they are manifesting divine presence. "Krishna Himself dances upon the tongue of one who utters His Name and in the ears of one who hears it. Krishna is present in the form of His Name whether you realise it or not" (Haddon, 2013: 258; emphasis removed). When chanted in public performance, the mantra follows a call-and-response form. Logically, writes Malcolm Haddon, this seems to organize the ritual around a speaker and a hearer; but, he notes, this interpretation would miss the point that speakers hear their own words, and although devoted chanters "may spiritually strive to 'own' the plea, to truly intend it ... the sound belongs to Krishna as His own body: the sound is Krishna Himself" (260; emphasis removed). In Hare Krishna theology, the distinction between representation and experience collapses in the transcendent purity of the divine name.[12]

Like sound, scent can signal a place's sacredness or sacralize by its presence. For example, the Ark of the Covenant was, on God's command, to be anointed with fragrant myrrh, cinnamon, calamus, and cassia in olive oil (Exodus 30: 23–25); in contrast, bad smells, "whether sulfurous or fecal ... announced Satan's continuing presence and its threat to the community" (Reinarz, 2014: 44). But, as with sound, it can be more productive to think about scent itself being the sacred site. In ancient Greece, the gods were "thought to enjoy feeding on the scents of burnt animal offerings," complementing the ambrosia and

---

[12] Hare Krishna theology leads Haddon to playfully interrogate anthropologists' understandings of how ethnography works. Noting that written forms of the divine name have inherent presence and force like chanted ones do, he observes that scholars' analyses of the Hare Krishna movement are inevitably acts of proselytization. To write about Hare Krishna is necessarily to do the movement's work (Haddon, 2013).

nectar they ate and with which they anointed themselves (Classen, Howes, and Synnott, 1994: 46). In twelfth-century England, a man described his vision of a deceased monk who "told how he was in Paradise and that there they lived off smell, which at the start of day descended from Heaven, satisfying and refreshing each according to his merits by a differential sweetness" (Woolgar, 2006: 119). As these examples suggest, smell's ephemerality and association with taste make it hard to isolate as a sacred site, and we do not want to stretch the concept of sacred space too far. Nonetheless, by infusing or permeating people and places, smell can become indissociable from their sacredness. For example, the "odor of sanctity" in early Christianity connected human and divine. "In early Christian tradition all priests were thought to emit a sweet odour in literal accordance with St. Paul's statement that 'we are the aroma of Christ to God among those who are being saved'" in 2 Corinthians 2: 15 (Classen, Howes, and Synnott, 1994: 52).[13]

Turning to taste and consumption, we note ambrosia, the food of the Greek gods; manna, which fell from heaven for the children of Israel; the bread and wine of the Eucharist, the body and blood of Christ. Food can both signify and manifest sacredness. Taste, as in the sensations of taste buds, can be a key feature: ambrosia tastes heavenly by definition, and manna is said to have tasted "like wafers made with honey" (Exodus 16: 31). In other cases, the act of consumption and the ritual logic it articulates matter more than sweetness (or any other flavor). For example, Christian communion creates a pattern of chiasmus (an X-shaped figure) in consumption – as people incorporate the body of Christ into themselves, they incorporate themselves into the body of Christ, understood as the Church. The beverage kava follows a similar semiotic pattern when consumed in Fiji. Kava is a shrub which farmers harvest, wash, air dry, and have pulverized. Kava powder is mixed into water and the dregs strained out, resulting in a mildly bitter and dusty-tasting beverage, also called kava (*yaqona* in Fijian). The serving of kava is the ritual centerpiece of many indigenous Fijian ceremonies, from chiefly installations to weddings and funerals (see Figure 9). Not to serve kava at an event might be taken as a sign that the event is not important. In drinking kava, one both incorporates the essence of the land and chiefly territory in which people's social identities are based (the *vanua*) and incorporates oneself into the *vanua* as social order (Tomlinson, 2014: 58–71).[14]

---

[13] Classen, Howes, and Synnott are quoting either the New Revised Standard Version or the English Standard Version. The King James Version is more evocative: "we are unto God a sweet savour of Christ, in them that are saved."

[14] We are suspending the question of whether ostensibly secular food can become an object of ritual devotion, as in haute cuisine that is described as transcendent; but we note with appreciation the

Figure 9 A highly ceremonial kava service in honor of paramount chiefs from Kadavu Island, Suva, Fiji, October 1998. Photo by Matt Tomlinson.

Sight may seem sensually overdetermined for experiencing the sacred. Whether humbled by a plain chapel or awed by a grand cathedral, whether luxuriating in religious iconography or insisting that particular subjects cannot be represented visually lest one blaspheme, seeing things as sacred is intrinsic to their being sacred. This logic achieves a kind of fullness in the Hindu practice of *darśan*, the seeing of sacred images and being seen by them. Diana L. Eck writes that in Hinduism, "seeing is a kind of touching" – a way of making contact – and also "a form of knowing" (1996: 9). When one looks at a divine image, one is worshiping by seeing the image, and the divinity inherent to the image "sees the worshiper as well. The contact between devotee and deity is exchanged through the eyes" (7). A key ritual moment in the fashioning of sacred images is when its eyes are "opened," for example by removing a coating of honey and ghee from them, or by placing "eyes" made of enamel into carved eye sockets (7, 53). "The gaze which falls from the newly-opened eyes of the deity," Eck reports, "is said to be so powerful that it must first fall upon some pleasing offering, such as sweets, or upon a mirror where it may see its own reflection. More than once has the tale been told of that powerful gaze falling upon some unwitting bystander, who died instantly of

---

lively analysis by Emily J. H. Contois (2015) of diet books as theological texts, with evil foods consumed immorally making one fat and sanctified foods consumed with discipline making one good. See also Christine Knight's (2012) entertaining analysis of the Atkins Diet as fundamentally Rousseauian, with nutritional and moral goodness alike rooted in the state of nature, and the South Beach Diet as a joyless Calvinist push for righteous self-denial. In both diets, refined carbohydrates are the Devil.

Making Places Sacred   41

its force" (7). Seeing is itself a sacred act, and vision is the sacred site, although Eck also describes India's elegant and elaborate traditions of designing and commemorating temples, villages, and the landscape: Emplacing the sacred, making sites for seeing. *Darśan*, in Eck's account, is a kind of creative visual dialogism.

No sense exists in isolation, and ethnographic descriptions of sacred practices can be sensational. Eck notes that a Hindu worshiper not only sees divinely, but also

> "touches" [the deity's image] with one's hands (*sparśa*), and ... also "touches" the limbs of one's own body to establish the presence of various deities (*nyāsa*). One "hears" the sacred sound of the *mantras* (*śravaṇa*). The ringing of bells, the offering of oil lamps, the presentation of flowers, the pouring of water and milk, the sipping of sanctified liquid offerings, the eating of consecrated food – these are the basic constituents of Hindu worship, *pūjā*. (Eck, 1996: 11–12)

Similarly, writing of Christians from the United States who go on Holy Land pilgrimages, Hillary Kaell points out that these trips are "a supremely sensory experience: stepping on ancient cobbled roads, shouldering a Cross along the Via Dolorosa, touching the tomb, and taking home twigs and rocks all contribute to making tangible Jesus's presence and his lived experience on earth" (2014: 16). One pilgrim mentions the story of doubting Thomas, to whom the wounded, resurrected Jesus said, "reach hither thy finger, and behold my hands; and reach hither thy hand, and thrust it into my side: and be not faithless, but believing" (John 20:27, King James Version). Kaell links it to her impulse to touch things on her journey: "If you can touch, you really know [Jesus] was real, he was here" (Kaell, 2014: 93; brackets in original). During a communion service at the Garden Tomb, another woman tells her pilgrimage group that her husband had died the previous year, but that she feels his presence here and now. This pilgrim "picked up stones throughout our trip, like most of our group," Kaell writes, adding that "these gained particular significance for her at the Mount of Olives, when she noticed the Jewish custom of leaving pebbles on graves. She brought back her favorite rocks for [her husband's] grave in North Carolina, thereby linking one presence-filled place with another" (93–4). The tangibility of the pilgrimage – this land we walk on, this desert heat, this cool garden with smooth stone surfaces – is an integral part of pilgrims' sense that they are in communion with the divine.

Writing of pilgrimages within Israel taken by Jews of South Asian heritage (Bene Israel), Gabriele Shenar describes "the sensory production, that is, how to listen, look, touch, move, chant, eat, pray, touch, and smell at each site, [which] clearly forms an important part of the pilgrimage experience" (2019: 125). Pilgrims ride through the dry and achingly hot landscape in comfortable buses, joking and chatting in Hebrew and Marathi, reciting Hebrew prayers set "to an Indian tune," playing Hindi-language Bollywood songs and Hebrew-language Qawwali ones, and filling the vehicle with the tantalizing aroma of Indian snacks (114). Shenar notes the separation of a spare Jewish-Israeli exterior and a cozy Indian interior during the bus rides, but also points out that the pilgrims work to create a culturally Indian ambiance at the sacred sites. A notable example is how, at the Cave of Elijah in Haifa, they ritually offer food to the prophet in a manner reminiscent of Hindu *puja* and *prasad* as well as Islamic practice (115).

In writing about the body as an especially vulnerable sacred site, we described how Spiritualist mediums connect their own bodily sensations with the ways people have died. If a medium feels pressure in her chest, she might take this to be a sign that the person communicating with her from the spirit world died of a heart attack. But mediums receive pleasant sensations, too – visions of people's faces; scents from their gardens; tastes from their kitchens; pleasant emotional warmth recalling a grandparent's love; and so forth. Because these sensations are within the medium's own mind and body, we identified the body as a sacred site in Spiritualist mediumship. In this section, however, we have urged closer consideration of senses themselves as loci. To turn from Spiritualism to another new religion, when Hare Krishna devotees chant a mantra, they are not commenting on divine presence: they are making it manifest, experiencing the divine in the sound itself. Wherever and whenever it is heard, "Hare Krishna, Hare Krishna, Krishna Krishna, Hare Hare, Hare Rama, Hare Rama, Rama Rama, Hare Hare" is the divine.

8 Sacred Space Can Be Unmade

One way to challenge preconceptions about sacred space is to ask, counterintuitively, what places are not sacred. We began this Element by describing the Spiritualist medium Norman Ivory's experiences at a park near the rail station in Bundanoon, New South Wales, Australia, precisely because for many people, this would not seem like a sacred space. If we wanted to see a giant archangel, we might go to a cathedral or a mountaintop: but, Bundanoon? For Norman, on that day and apparently to his own surprise, the answer was: yes, Bundanoon. Yet we have to acknowledge that some places seem notably disenchanted, and some places are actively desacralized.

Within the broad topic of desacralization, it is crucial to distinguish between desecration (the violation of sacredness) and deconsecration (the respectful reclassification of something as no longer sacred), and to distinguish both of these from a foundational condition of non-sacredness.

Desecration or iconoclasm is perhaps the easiest to understand intuitively. People defile or profane a space that others hold sacred in order to show that it is not really sacred after all. The methods are various, and sometimes spectacular. Elijah challenges the prophets of Baal to see whose sacrifice will be divinely accepted, as recounted in 1 Kings 18. The monk Columbanus blows on an enormous barrel of beer dedicated to Woden to make it burst. A Solomon Islands Christian evangelist named Solomon Damusoe climbs a supposedly sacred mountain to prove he will not suffer for having tread upon it (Tomlinson, 2017). In cases like these and countless more, evangelical agents violate local expectations of how the sacred should be treated in order to suggest that there is a different and better way to understand sacredness.

Debra McDougall's (2016) work on Christianity and sociality in Ranongga, Solomon Islands, reveals lively and ongoing contests between sacralization and desacralization. Villagers recall a mid-twentieth century Methodist pastor named Boazi Nunukujuku who had "an almost crazy faith in God," a faith he expressed by repeatedly challenging traditional anxieties about sacredness. "Wherever there were dangerous devils," McDougall recalls being told by one man in 2000, "that was where old Boazi would make his garden or plant his copra." Unfazed by a coastal area's reputation as the "coast of the dead," Boazi called it the "coast of people" and developed a coconut plantation there (106). He hedged his bets slightly when confronting a wooden figure in a shrine that was considered especially powerful: Boazi addressed the figure, saying he would return in three days if he did not fall sick before then. He remained healthy. So Boazi gathered some plantation laborers, went back to the shrine, and mocked the wooden "idol" by ceremonially offering it dirt. He then lit it on fire. As one man recalled, "he killed it completely" (106–7).

McDougall notes that at the time of her research, different Christian denominations treated traditional sacred space differently. United Church members were cautious. When one man took her and other visitors to a shrine complex, he was on the lookout for signs of how the ancestral spirits felt about this. For example, when a snake lying across the path slithered away, the man understood this as permission to proceed. In contrast to United Church members' wariness, Seventh-day Adventists were unconcerned. Indeed, one Adventist man told McDougall to climb onto a boulder where skulls were kept, ostensibly so she could pull moss away from a carving in the stone. What she was told to do, she writes, intentionally showed

> disregard of the customary pattern whereby the sacred was associated with men and kept separate from and above women's bodies. John Matepitu told me not to worry: there is not a single place around Modo where a woman

cannot go, no ancestral powers to be avoided. All people are now completely free to go where they wish. (McDougall, 2016: 111–12)

McDougall was respectful of Ranonggan religiosity, and realized that the action she was told to take would be interpreted as evidence of ancestral spirits' powerlessness.

Deconsecration works differently than desecration for the obvious reason that it is a respectful act. On November 12, 2017, the Dominican Church in Münster, Germany, was ceremonially deconsecrated (Radermacher, 2021). An auxiliary bishop conducted the final worship service, declaring that after this day, the building would "not be a church anymore." He quoted from the third chapter of Ecclesiastes, which begins, "To every thing there is a season, and a time to every purpose under the heaven." He spoke performatively, reciting the Church's "decree of profanation." Candles and the sanctuary lamp were extinguished, the altar cloth removed, and the consecrated host taken to a nearby church, materially marking the end of an era – a closure apparently made final when the last priest to exit the church closed the doors and placed "a large symbolic 'X'" on them (6–7). The next year, a Foucault's pendulum made by the artist Gerhard Richter was installed, making the space a site for public art.[15]

Martin Radermacher writes that to think of the church building as having long been sacred and now suddenly not sacred would be to overlook its complicated history, which included its being used as a military installation from 1826 to 1880 and having hosted art exhibitions before Richter showed up (2021: 3, 16–18). Indeed, considering the church's history of construction, renovation, and transformation, the auxiliary bishop stated at the deconsecration service that it was "not completely unlikely that it might even be consecrated again one day" (7).[16]

A trickier topic than desacralization is foundational non-sacredness, or places that have never been sacred. To anticipate our argument in the next section, sacred space reaffirms the human. Places that have not had any human inhabitants, or no long-term human settlement, are in a category of their own – unless one reverts to a theological assertion that all of creation is divine. Rather than witness the unmaking of sacred space, such places are metaphorical blank slates; they have no indigenous populations to claim original connections and no deep-time ruins to starkly juxtapose death with living continuity.

---

[15] Richter did not endear himself to church leaders when he mentioned that by installing the device that disproved geocentrism, "a 'small victory of the natural sciences over the church'" had been won (Radermacher, 2021: 19).

[16] As the geographer Veronica della Dora (2018: 55) affirms, "Desacralization is . . . often followed by resacralization." She proposes to study sacred space in terms of "infrasecular" dynamics wherein "the secular and the religious coexist, overlap and compete" and desacralization and resacralization are never fully separate processes (2018: 48, 54–8).

Consider Antarctica. Is Antarctica sacred? As we wrote at the beginning of this Element, because sacredness is a value, the analytical question is always: sacred for whom? Many tourists go to Antarctica to encounter "nature as a distanced, mythical, and magical world of purity, origin, and divine forms" (Picard, 2015: 307–8). Such tourists have already made Antarctica a sacred space before arriving. The scientists and military personnel who work there might seem to have a secular bent, but nevertheless eight Christian houses of worship have been established on the icy continent: an American chapel that hosts both Protestant and Catholic services; four Catholic chapels (one nestled in an ice cave); and three Eastern Orthodox sites, two identified as chapels and one as a church (Frye, 2022). To a distant observer, Antarctica might seem to be foundationally non-sacred, but many people are at work actively sacralizing it. Indeed, beyond the churches stand numerous informal shrines. "Perhaps the most famous shrine on Antarctica," writes Ellen C. Frye, "is affectionately known as Roll Cage Mary, at McMurdo Station. This statue of the Virgin Mary ... inside a steel cage to protect her from the Antarctic weather, is perched on a hill overlooking the research station, watching over the people currently working there and over the souls of those whose lives were lost during the construction of the station" (123).

The topic of non-sacredness requires consideration of pollution. In stating this, we acknowledge that pollution is a complicated topic because it can be a mark of spiritual presence. Consider Charles Stafford's (2010) story of his earnest attempts to learn about local ritual practices in Angang, Taiwan. He attended a funeral and was excited by how much he learned. When a second funeral took place, he went eagerly and was even asked to carry a parcel of offerings, including food, to the burial site. This seemed like great anthropological fortune – to observe fascinating rituals and, even better, to be invited to participate. But Stafford learned that locals felt he had become spiritually polluted by his actions. A shopkeeper friend took him to see a spirit medium to be cleansed, but also asked that Stafford not touch the religious objects in her shop lest customers refuse to buy them as a result. People also instructed him to stop attending funerals. Stafford learned to his discomfort and frustration that in attempting to behave ethically as a researcher, he had become spiritually toxic. His story points to the vulnerability of bodies, which we discussed earlier, and opens up the question of sacredness' ethical alignment: the power of the dead was working through the well-meaning anthropologist, and although many locals understood that he meant no harm, they still worried about what kind of spiritual effect he might transmit.

But visitors, in turn, might be discomfited by the material pollution they encounter at sacred sites. Joshua Nash (2012), a linguist and anthropologist who describes himself as an "environmentalist–pilgrim," notes the destructive dynamic of religious tourism in Vrindavan, northern India. The 500-year-old town is famous for its beautiful forest groves and meadows, and is a popular site for pilgrims who come to worship Krishna. But, Nash observes, so many pilgrims now come and stay that many groves and meadows have been parceled out to developers, and the town itself is crowded and suffering from challenges of waste disposal. Krishna devotees, other than Nash, do not necessarily draw a direct connection between environmental damage and challenges to the sacred. Indeed, he describes the paradox wherein Vrindavan as a specific place points to Krishna's universal emplacement: "the actual location of Vrindavan provides the understanding that any place or environment, when perceived with awareness of its inherent divinity, is Vrindavan" (109). Yet he ruefully quotes an author who points out that pilgrims who show up to see the divine in forests and ponds now sometimes feel "despair" rather than fulfilment when seeing what those forests and ponds have become (108).

Our point is simply to note that just as sacredness is a project of human evaluation, so are challenges to asserted sacredness – whether iconoclastic or reverential, intentional or unintentional, purely imaginative or stonily practical. Without wanting to reduce the dazzling endeavors of sacred space-making to a crude binary structure, we nonetheless emphasize that concepts of sacred space only make sense when one recognizes or defines other spaces as not sacred, for whatever reason.

9 Sacred Space Reaffirms the Human

If anyone is notably *uninterested* in sacred space, it might seem to be those who explicitly declare themselves not to be religious or spiritual. Celebrants in the British Humanist Association conduct funerals for people who, their descendants affirm, did not care about things like church or God while they were alive (Engelke, 2015). Because humanist funeral services are often conducted in multi-purpose chapels with dominantly Christian iconography, Matthew Engelke observes, a preliminary task for many celebrants is to cover up or remove as much of the religious symbolism as they can before the event begins. Celebrants do not offer prayers, and do not declare that the deceased is now in heaven.

Engelke notes that there is a stubborn problem inherent to humanist funeral services – what one celebrant calls "the elephant in the room" (Engelke, 2015: 41). It is the coffin, and the body inside of it, standing in stark prominence and needing to be acknowledged in some way. This is clearly not just a wooden box with organic matter inside it, but something much more significant, indeed the reason we are all gathered here today. How, exactly, is it significant in a tradition that resolutely rejects sacralization?

A key ethnographic moment comes from a service during which the celebrant, Johnny, "walked over to the coffin, still on the catafalque, and touched it, very gently, as he might touch the shoulder of a person" (Engelke, 2015: 31). This moment seemed remarkable to another humanist celebrant who was present, Sophie, because celebrants usually do not touch coffins, worried that to call attention to coffins and their bodies would unsettle the determinedly nonreligious nature of the service. "The reluctance or refusal to touch the coffin is best seen not in terms of the body's profanity," Engelke writes, "but, rather, sacrality, or at least, its recognition as something special. Humanists in the [British Humanist Association] might want a closed world structure, but this does not preclude the possibility of recognizing certain ideas and objects as in some sense sacred" (43). Dead bodies, as we have noted, often lend themselves to projects of sacralization. Johnny's lightly touching the coffin "impressed" Sophie as a deft ritual action, she said, because he had acknowledged the presence of the dead body in a "very, very natural" way. He softened the threat of the sacred within the humanist frame (41). Dead bodies are sacred, but one does not need to invoke the sacred to deal with them respectfully.

Engelke focuses on coffins and bodies for their material inescapability, but another way to read his account of humanist funerals is as a reaffirmation of humanity and sociality as sacred – an ironic affirmation for people who downplay signs of the sacred as much as possible. It is an anthropological truism that people make God and gods in their own image, in opposition to the theological claim that God has shaped humanity in the divine image. Both readings, the secular–anthropological and the theological, join humanity and divinity in a significant way.

If Mircea Eliade overstated the universality of a sacred axis linking underworld, earth, and heaven, his attention to "hierophany" remains useful in some ways. Hierophany, or sacredness made manifest, is the quality people seek and find in the spaces we have discussed in this Element. We have looked to loci as varied as museums and internet sites, dead bodies and birdsong, puffs of smoke and place names, in addition to more readily recognizable sacred spaces like inner sanctums and pilgrimage sites. To adapt Gertrude Stein's famous jest about Oakland, California, as having "no there there," sacred spaces necessarily have a "there" there, a quality which indexes extrahuman presence.

Hierophany always requires an act of recognition, a subject who sees, hears, smells, tastes, touches, or intuits a sign as an index of sacredness. This might sound like circular reasoning: people make the sacred; therefore, the sacred is made by people. Rather than get stuck in a logical loop like this, we want to point out how sacred space reaffirms the human by calling attention to the extrahuman – the ghosts, reanimated ancestors, nature spirits, gods, and souls that people seek and find in so many places. Those places include geographic locations, virtual realities, and imagined worlds. No space is inherently sacred, and no space is sacred for everyone, but all sacred spaces affirm humanity's ability to go beyond ourselves existentially.

Humanity is a spectacularly diverse constellation of social possibilities, and when people engage with others who are starkly different from themselves, they often turn those counterparts into either gods or monsters – awe-inspiring or repellent examples of how truly different people can be (Stasch, 2016). So, too, different sacred spaces feature different kinds of extrahumanity. Jonathan Edwards's notorious 1741 sermon "Sinners in the Hands of an Angry God" spends much time describing the fires of hell, wherein devils (and the Devil) wait to pounce on new arrivals. Edwards's vision is severe and unrelenting:

> That world of misery, that lake of burning brimstone is extended abroad under you. There is the dreadful pit of the glowing flames of the wrath of God; there is hell's wide gaping mouth open; and you have nothing to stand upon, nor anything to take hold of: there is nothing between you and hell but the air; 'tis only the power and mere pleasure of God that holds you up. (Kimnach, Minkema, and Sweeney, 1999: 55)

These words contrast sharply with reports from Spiritualist mediums about the calm and gentle nature of the afterlife most people will encounter. When the respected British physicist Sir Oliver J. Lodge sat with the medium Gladys Osborne Leonard on December 3, 1915, he heard – as he expected – from his son Raymond, who had recently been killed in the Great War. Raymond said through Mrs. Leonard that people in the spirit world "try to provide everything that is wanted." He said that a man had wanted a cigar, which Raymond had doubted would be possible to procure in the afterlife. To his surprise, the man got one – or at least a passable substitute: "there are laboratories over here, and they manufacture all sorts of things in them. Not like you do, out of solid matter, but out of essences, and ethers, and gases. It's not the same as on the earth plane, but they were able to manufacture what looked like a cigar." Other residents in the spirit world, Raymond added, "want meat, and some strong drink; they call for whisky sodas." After a few cigars or a couple of drinks, Raymond explained, the desire for these kinds of things wanes (Lodge, 1916: 197–8). Another stout Spiritualist, Sir Arthur Conan Doyle, gave lectures on its philosophy. A historian describes his view of life after death: "Golf, he thought, was likely to be played. In fact, Conan Doyle's Heaven was rather like Sussex, slightly watered down" (Brandon, 1983: 222).

It might sound odd to refer to both a Puritan preacher's idea of hell and a Spiritualist medium's idea of a tastefully bland afterlife as sacred spaces. Do they really belong in the same analytical frame as the Shikoku pilgrimage circuit, the Kaluli longhouse during a séance, or the Ethiopian coffee forest and its demanding taboos and ritual schedules? Our answer is yes, they do, because they all sacralize space in order to reaffirm the human. We say "reaffirm" because humans are the ones doing the affirming, and in describing and engaging with these sacred spaces, they are using ideas of the extrahuman to reconsider the human.

We offer a final example of sacred space, one which brings together many of the themes discussed in the preceding pages. In 2010, the Bishop Museum of Honolulu held an exhibit of the only three remaining statues in the world of Kū, the Hawaiian deity "most famously (and reductively) known as 'the god of war,'" more aptly described as "the deity of male generative power" (Tengan, 2016: 57). The statues, carved from breadfruit trees, weigh 800 pounds each. Only one stood in the Bishop Museum before the exhibit opened; the other two were at Salem, Massachusetts' Peabody Essex Museum and the British Museum in London. Bringing them together required a great deal of time, planning, and money, and staff at both the Peabody Essex and British Museum were anxious that sending them to Hawai'i might provoke claims for repatriation.

The most challenging aspect of bringing the carved statues into the same space – which was to be the first time in almost 200 years that three Kū images stood together anywhere – was the fact that *mana* was at stake. *Mana*, a term found in many Oceanic languages, can loosely and provisionally be translated as "spiritual power," although it can play several grammatical roles and its range of meanings varies considerably by language and context of speaking (Tomlinson and Tengan, 2016). People commenting on the reunification of three Kū images translated *mana* as "belonging" and "status" as well as "spiritual power" (Tengan, 2016: 56). On one level, bringing the three Kū together was evidently a manifestation of indigenous Hawaiian sovereignty as an NRM – a way of effectively linking god, people, and place, reasserting indigenous heritage and belonging. On another level, considering Kū's masculinity, the union of Kū images was specifically a statement about men's position and authority in Hawai'i, an articulation of male significance in a culture with prominent female aesthetics and power; indeed, whose last reigning monarch was a queen, Lili'uokalani. The team that oversaw the movement of the Kū images from Salem and London to Honolulu and back again were members of an indigenous Hawaiian men's group that practiced traditional martial arts and had served in the US military – the ideal men to guard and be guarded by Kū.

A key story about Kū is that he was originally human, and when his family was starving, "he told his wife that he could save them only if he went on a journey from which he could not return" (Tengan, 2016: 55). He stood on his head and sank into the ground. His grieving wife's tears at that site brought forth the breadfruit tree whose fruit saved everyone. The story gives emotional resonance to the life stories of the Hawaiian men's group members. One, Billy Kahalepuna Richards, had intentionally claimed Kū as his god when he went to fight in the Vietnam War. He survived the war and, decades later, was asked to substitute for his brother in-law, who was unable to join the trip to return the Kū images back to Salem and London. Richards was not sure he could or should, until his wife remarked, "Kū took you through war. Maybe it's time to thank him" (64).

The Kū figures, sacred in themselves for many indigenous Hawaiians as representations of divinity, were even more intensely sacred in being united in their homeland of Hawai'i. But this sacredness made some people anxious. As the Bishop Museum's project director recalled, "You have an older, more conservative Hawaiian group that were *fearful*. So, what happens when the three [Kū] come together? What about the mana, or energy that might be *re*-animated? ... Who's responsible if you *awaken* something?" (Noelle Kahanu quoted in Tengan, 2016: 58; emphasis in original). Others were less worried, seeing the intensification of *mana* as a blessing. "When you go in" to the museum space, said renowned tattoo master Keone Nunes,

> you don't feel that you're fearful for your life, but you can feel the mana of these images in a very welcoming way, in a very heartfelt way.... There's a lot of things that it can represent for each and every one of us ... who come and see these images for something that is beyond the carved image, beyond the wood. (Quoted in Tengan, 2016: 60)

What is in and beyond the Kū images is *mana*, and that *mana* is deeply human-affirming because of its extrahuman qualities. Kū was originally a human, and his collective return as three united images both motivates and reflects people's desires for, variously, recognition of indigenous sovereignty, pride in masculinity, and potential for the collective generation of new *mana*. Indeed, the Bishop Museum included in its 2010 annual report a guestbook comment in which a visitor suggested that the *mana* of Kū was manifest precisely in the way people had come together in harmony to see the images united.

Here was a conjunction of multiple sacred spaces: individual carved images of divinity placed alongside each other within the museum as a site for honoring indigenous Hawaiian knowledge, practices, and values. The figures coming from Salem and London were not pilgrims – they were coming home, although they did return to Salem and London after the exhibit closed. The men accompanying the figures on their journeys were not quite pilgrims, either, but saw themselves as warriors with a sanctified purpose. Visitors to the museum were made aware that this was a momentous event in a unique space, the first time three Kū stood together in almost two hundred years. Here, then, was the creation of sacred space, and reflection upon it, in a deeply moving and elegantly human register of connection, belonging, and hope.

Conclusion

At the beginning of this Element, we referred to Jonathan Z. Smith's argument that sacredness "is, above all, a category of emplacement" (1987: 104). We also mentioned Hannen Swaffer's complaint that people would accept "evidence of the hereafter" from the New Testament even though they had no knowledge of how the text was written – "It must take place in Jerusalem to convince you, not Kingston Vale" (1962: 5). To close this loop of reference, we can return to Smith's blunt claim about what, for millions of people, is the most sacred space on earth: "There is nothing inherent in the location of the Temple in Jerusalem. Its location was simply where it happened to be built" (1987: 83).

Smith is not a lighthearted author, but his words here sound almost comically dismissive. "Nothing inherent" – the phrase might seem to wave away sacredness. "Simply where it happened" – a matter of contingency. And yet, following his reasoning, we have here worked to show how this understanding of sacred space-making is both accurate and compelling for our understandings of how humans work to connect with the extrahuman.

New Religious Movements are fertile sites for investigating the novel and creative ways people make places sacred. In this Element, we have used examples from a wide array of NRMs, including Spiritualism, Krishna Consciousness, a millenarian movement in the Solomon Islands, Peoples Temple (Jonestown), religious tourism, and an indigenous sovereignty movement. These examples' eclecticism is to the point: Any group making a claim to connect with the extrahuman needs to make that connection somewhere. The "somewhere" can be a geographic site, but it can also be a body, a sound, or an imaginative space. The dynamism of NRMs is seen in the active sacralization of a wide range of possible places. We have taken care to note, too, that mainstream, long-established religious groups also do the ongoing work of defining sacred space.

In recognizing that sacredness is a value, the question "sacred for whom?" is always a productive one for research. Our approach in this Element has been expansive, but it has not been a free-for-all, we hope. Recall the point that some spaces need to markedly *not* be sacred for others to be so. We have shown that sacred space can be associated with blood, death, and natural features in networks of sites whose auras enhance each other, but that no feature is determinative. Above all, human action makes sacred space, and this work reaffirms humanity by connecting with extrahuman figures. Affirmations of humanity can be concentrated in people's bodies as sacred spaces, but bodies are also more vulnerable to insult and loss than other sites. Sacred space is multidimensional and multisensory, meaning it can be made almost anywhere – Bundanoon, Tavuki, Nagasaki, Sāmoa, Antarctica, a room off a crowded airport corridor, online, the sound of a chanted mantra – but it can also be unmade. Unmaking sacred space can be an iconoclastic move of *new* sacralization: goodbye to the temple, hello to the church; goodbye to the church, hello to the mosque. But it can also simply end with the unmaking, a formerly sacred site now not treated as such by most people.

References

Ahdar, R. T. 2013. Samoa and the Christian State Ideal. *International Journal for the Study of the Christian Church* 13(1): 59–72.

Ames, M. M. 1992. *Cannibal Tours and Glass Boxes: The Anthropology of Museums*. Vancouver: UBC Press.

Anderson, B. 1991. *Imagined Communities: Reflections on the Origin and Spread of Nationalism*, rev. and extended ed. London: Verso.

Arcones, P. C. 2012. *Sons of Heaven, Brothers of Nature: The Naxi of Southwest China*. Kunming: Papers of the White Dragon.

Arno, A. 1990. Disentangling Indirectly: The Joking Debate in Fijian Social Control. In *Disentangling: Conflict Discourse in Pacific Societies*, ed. K. A. Watson-Gegeo and G. M. White, pp. 241–89. Stanford, CA: Stanford University Press.

Asad, T. 1999. Religion, Nation-State, Secularism. In *Nation and Religion: Perspectives on Europe and Asia*, ed. P. van der Veer and H. Lehmann, pp. 178–96. Princeton, NJ: Princeton University Press.

Asad, T. 2003. *Formations of the Secular: Christianity, Islam, Modernity*. Stanford, CA: Stanford University Press.

Austin, J. L. 1975. *How to Do Things with Words*, 2nd ed., ed. J. O. Urmson and M. Sbisà. Cambridge, MA: Harvard University Press.

Barrera, A. 1991. Mexican-American Roadside Crosses in Starr County. In *Hecho en Tejas: Texas-Mexican Folk Arts and Crafts*, ed. J. S. Graham, pp. 278–92. Denton, TX: University of North Texas Press.

Basso, K. H. 1996. *Wisdom Sits in Places: Landscape and Language among the Western Apache*. Albuquerque, NM: University of New Mexico Press.

Berger, S. and C. Tekin, eds. 2018. *History and Belonging: Representations of the Past in Contemporary European Politics*. New York: Berghahn Books.

Berns, S. 2016. Considering the Glass Case: Material Encounters between Museums, Visitors, and Religious Objects. *Journal of Material Culture* 21(2): 153–68.

Blum, S. D. 2001. *Portraits of "Primitives": Ordering Human Kinds in the Chinese Nation*. Lanham, MD: Rowman & Littlefield.

Boylston, T. 2018. *The Stranger at the Feast: Prohibition and Mediation in an Ethiopian Orthodox Christian Community*. Berkeley, CA: University of California Press.

Brandon, R. 1983. *The Spiritualists: The Passion for the Occult in the Nineteenth and Twentieth Centuries*. London: Weidenfeld and Nicolson.

Benjamin, W. 2008. The Work of Art in the Age of Its Technological Reproducibility: Second Version. In *The Work of Art in the Age of Its Technological Reproducibility, and Other Writings on Media*, ed. M. W. Jennings, B. Doherty, and T. Y. Levin, pp. 19–55. Cambridge, MA: The Belknap Press of Harvard University Press.

Brown, D. 2016. Context and Experiencing the Sacred. *Royal Institute of Philosophy Supplement* 79: 117–132.

Brulon Soares, B. 2019. Every Museum Has a God, or God Is in Every Museum? *ICOFOM Study Series* 47(1–2): 57–72.

Butler, J. 1990. *Gender Trouble: Feminism and the Subversion of Identity*. New York: Routledge.

Cadge, W. 2018. The Evolution of American Airport Chapels: Local Negotiations in Religiously Pluralistic Contexts. *Religion and American Culture* 28(1): 135–65.

Campbell, H. A., ed. 2013. *Digital Religion: Understanding Religious Practice in New Media Worlds*. Abingdon: Routledge.

Cannell, F. 1999. *Power and Intimacy in the Christian Philippines*. Cambridge: Cambridge University Press.

Chao, E. K. 1995. Depictions of Difference: History, Gender, Ritual and State Discourse among the Naxi of Southwest China. Ph.D. diss., University of Michigan.

Chao, E. K. 2012. *Lijiang Stories: Shamans, Taxi Drivers, and Runaway Brides in Reform-Era China*. Seattle, WA: University of Washington Press.

Chau, A. Y. 2011. Modalities of Doing Religion and Ritual Polytropy: Evaluating the Religious Market Model from the Perspective of Chinese Religious History. *Religion* 41(4): 547–68.

Chen, H-H. 2014. The Making of an Exotic Homeland: Performing Place, Identity and Belonging on China's Southwest Borderland. Ph.D. diss., The University of Wisconsin – Madison.

Classen, C., D. Howes, and A. Synnott. 1994. *Aroma: The Cultural History of Smell*. London: Routledge.

Cohen, E. 1988. Authenticity and Commoditization in Tourism. *Annals of Tourism Research* 15(3): 371–86.

Coleman, S. 2000. *The Globalisation of Charismatic Christianity*. Cambridge: Cambridge University Press.

Coleman, S. 2022. *Powers of Pilgrimage: Religion in a World of Movement*. New York: New York University Press.

Collins, C. O. and C. D. Rhine. 2003. Roadside Memorials. *OMEGA* 47(3): 221–44.

Contois, E. J. H. 2015. Guilt-Free and Sinfully Delicious: A Contemporary Theology of Weight Loss Dieting. *Fat Studies* 4(2): 112–26.

Connelly, L. 2013. Virtual Buddhism: Buddhist Ritual in Second Life. In *Digital Religion: Understanding Religious Practice in New Media Worlds*, ed. H. A. Campbell, pp. 128–35. Abingdon: Routledge.

Croke, B. 2022. *Flashpoint Hagia Sophia*. London: Routledge.

Dawkins, R. 2004. The Sacred and the Scientist. In *Is Nothing Sacred?*, ed. B. Rogers, pp. 135–7. London: Routledge.

Dawson, L. and D. Cowan. 2004. *Religion Online: Finding Faith on the Internet*. New York: Routledge.

della Dora, V. 2018. Infrasecular Geographies: Making, Unmaking and Remaking Sacred Space. *Progress in Human Geography* 42(1): 44–71.

Denton, K. A. 2014. *Exhibiting the Past: Historical Memory and the Politics of Museums in Postsocialist China*. Honolulu, HI: University of Hawai'i Press.

Discipleship Ministries, United Methodist Church. 2013 [1992]. A Service for the Consecration or Reconsecration of a Church Building. Nashville, TN: Discipleship Ministries. www.umcdiscipleship.org/book-of-worship/a-service-for-the-consecration-or-reconsecration-of-a-church-building, accessed August 7, 2024.

Duncan, C. 1995. *Civilizing Rituals: Inside Public Art Museums*. London: Routledge.

Eck, D. L. 1996. *Darśan: Seeing the Divine Image in India*, 2nd ed. New York: Columbia University Press.

Edwards, H. and R. Branch. 1974. *A Guide to the Understanding and Practice of Spiritual Healing*. Guildford: The Healer.

Efi, His Highness Tui Atua T. T. T. 2014. Whispers and Vanities in Samoan Indigenous Religious Culture. In *Whispers and Vanities: Samoan Indigenous Knowledge and Religion*, ed. T. M. Suaalii-Sauni, Maualaivao A. Wendt, V. Mo'a, et al., pp. 11–41. Wellington, New Zealand: Huia.

El Antably, A. H. 2011. Experiencing the Past: The Virtual (Re)Construction of Places. Ph.D. diss., University of California, Berkeley.

Eliade, M. 1961[1957]. *The Sacred and the Profane: The Nature of Religion*, trans. W. R. Trask. New York: Harper and Brothers.

Emmett, C. F. 2009. The Siting of Churches and Mosques as an Indicator of Christian–Muslim Relations. *Islam and Christian–Muslim Relations* 20(4): 451–76.

Engelke, M. 2015. The Coffin Question: Death and Materiality in Humanist Funerals. *Material Religion* 11(1): 26–48.

Engelke, M. 2021. Some Moods and Modes of Enchantment in the Human Sciences: On the Troublesome Dead. *Religion* 51(4): 551–65.

Everett, H. 2002. *Roadside Crosses in Contemporary Memorial Culture.* Denton, TX: University of North Texas Press.

Feld, S. 1982. *Sound and Sentiment: Birds, Weeping, Poetics, and Song in Kaluli Expression.* Philadelphia, PA: University of Pennsylvania Press.

Feld, S. 1996. Waterfalls of Song: An Acoustemology of Place Resounding in Bosavi, Papua New Guinea. In *Senses of Place*, ed. S. Feld and K. H. Basso, pp. 91–135. Santa Fe, NM: School of American Research Press.

Fleeson, N. E. 2023. "Not Built as a Shrine, but as a Sacred Space": The Devotional Nature of Museums Dedicated to Candidates for Sainthood. *Material Religion* 19(3): 284–304.

Fox, J. J. 2014. Turn Right at the Buddha. In *The Coombs: A House of Memories*, 2nd ed., ed. B. V. Lal and A. Ley, pp. 61–6. Canberra: ANU Press.

Frye, E. C. 2022. The Ant-Architecture of Religion and Spirituality in Antarctica. In *Antarcticness: Inspirations and Imaginaries*, ed. I. Kelman, pp. 115–28. London: UCL Press.

Gieryn, T. F. 2018. *Truth-Spots: How Places Make People Believe.* Chicago, IL: University of Chicago Press.

Goullart, P. 1955. *Forgotten Kingdom.* London: John Murray.

Greenspan, E. L. 2006. Scaling Tragedy: Memorialization and Globalization at the World Trade Center Site. Ph.D. diss., University of Pennsylvania.

Grim, B. J., T. M. Johnson, V. Skirbekk, and G. A. Zurlo. 2014. *Yearbook of International Religious Demography 2014.* Leiden: Brill.

Grimes, R. L. 1992. Sacred Objects in Museum Spaces. *Studies in Religion/Sciences Religieuses* 21(4): 419–30.

Guinn, J. 2017. *The Road to Jonestown: Jim Jones and Peoples Temple.* New York: Simon & Schuster.

Haddon, M. 2013. Anthropological Proselytism: Reflexive Questions for a Hare Krishna Ethnography. *The Australian Journal of Anthropology* 24(3): 250–69.

Harrison, R. P. 2003. *The Dominion of the Dead.* Chicago, IL: University of Chicago Press.

Hartig, K. V. and K. M. Dunn. 1998. Roadside Memorials: Interpreting New Deathscapes in Newcastle, New South Wales. *Australian Geographical Studies* 36(1): 5–20.

Harvey, T. 2006. Sacred Spaces, Common Places: The Cemetery in the Contemporary American City. *The Geographical Review* 96(2): 295–312.

Hayes, C. 2021. The Spiritual in the Mundane: The Poetry of the Shikoku O-Henro Pilgrimage. In *Sacred Sites and Sacred Stories across Cultures: Transmission of Oral Tradition, Myth, and Religiosity*, ed. D. W. Kim, pp. 191–223. Cham: Palgrave Macmillan.

Hemingway, D. 1993. "Into All the World": Tala Samoa. Published Privately; Copy in University of Auckland Library, Auckland, New Zealand.

Henzel, C. 1991. *Cruces* in the Roadside Landscape of Northeastern Mexico. *Journal of Cultural Geography* 11(2): 93–106.

Hill-Smith, C. 2011. Cyberpilgrimage: The (Virtual) Reality of Online Pilgrimage Experience. *Religion Compass* 5(6): 236–46.

Inoue, N. 2000. From Religious Conformity to Innovation: New Ideas of Religious Journey and Holy Places. *Social Compass* 47(1): 21–32.

Ivory, N. 2016. *The Rabbit on the Roof: Man's Spiritual Life – A Discovery Adventure*. Bloomington, IN: Balboa Press.

Ivy, M. 1995. *Discourses of the Vanishing: Modernity, Phantasm, Japan*. Chicago, IL: University of Chicago Press.

Jacobs, S. 2007. Virtually Sacred: The Performance of Asynchronous Cyber-Rituals in Online Spaces. *Journal of Computer-Mediated Communication* 12(3): 1103–21.

Jang, K. 2020. Creating the Sacred Places of Pop Culture in the Age of Mobility: Fan Pilgrimages and Authenticity through Performance. *Journal of Tourism and Cultural Change* 18(1): 42–57.

Jones, R. D. 2019. The Makeshift and the Contingent: Lefebvre and the Production of Precarious Sacred Space. *Environment and Planning D: Society and Space* 37(1): 177–94.

Kaell, H. 2014. *Walking Where Jesus Walked: American Christians and Holy Land Pilgrimage*. New York: New York University Press.

Kalvig, A. 2017. *The Rise of Contemporary Spiritualism: Concepts and Controversies in Talking to the Dead*. London: Routledge.

Kang, X. 2009. Two Temples, Three Religions, and a Tourist Attraction: Contesting Sacred Space on China's Ethnic Frontier. *Modern China* 35(3): 227–55.

Kempf, W. 2019. Between Land and Horizon: Assemblages of Beings, Places and Things in Kiribati. In *Haunted Pacific: Anthropologists Investigate Spectral Apparitions across Oceania*, ed. R. I. Lohmann, pp. 118–42. Durham, NC: Carolina Academic Press.

Kimnach, W. H., K. P. Minkema, and D. A. Sweeney, eds. 1999. *The Sermons of Jonathan Edwards: A Reader*. New Haven, CT: Yale University Press.

Klaassens, M., P. Groote, and P. P. P. Huigen. 2009. Roadside Memorials from a Geographical Perspective. *Mortality* 14(2): 187–201.

Knight, C. 2012. "An Alliance with Mother Nature": Natural Food, Health, and Morality in Low-Carbohydrate Diet Books. *Food and Foodways* 20(2): 102–22.

Kong, L. 2001. Mapping "New" Geographies of Religion: Politics and Poetics in Modernity. *Progress in Human Geography* 25(2): 211–33.

Kong, L. 2005. Re-Presenting the Religious: Nation, Community and Identity in Museums: Re-Présenter Le Religieux: La Nation, La Communauté et l'Identité Dans Les Musées. *Social & Cultural Geography* 6(4): 495–513.

Kulick, D. 2003. No. *Language and Communication* 23(2): 139–51.

Lal, B. V. 2014. The Coombs: Journeys and Transformations. In *The Coombs: A House of Memories*, 2nd ed., ed. B. V. Lal and A. Ley, pp. 1–26. Canberra: ANU Press.

Lal, B. V. and A. Ley, eds. 2014. *The Coombs: A House of Memories*, 2nd ed. Canberra: ANU Press.

Li, G. 1997. *Dictionary of Dongba Culture*. Kunming: Yunnan Education Press.

Lodge, Sir O. J. 1916. *Raymond, or Life and Death: With Examples of the Evidence for Survival of Memory and Affection after Death*. New York: George H. Doran.

Macdonald, S. 2005. Enchantment and Its Dilemmas: The Museum as a Ritual Site. In *Science, Magic and Religion: The Ritual Processes of Museum Magic*, ed. M. Bouquet and N. Porto, pp. 209–28. Oxford: Berghahn Books.

Macdonald, S. 2013. *Memory Lands: Heritage and Identity in Europe Today*. Abingdon: Routledge.

Macdonald, S. 2015. Is "Difficult Heritage" Still "Difficult"? Why Public Acknowledgment of Past Perpetration May No Longer Be So Unsettling to Collective Identities. *Museum International* 67(1–4): 6–22.

MacWilliams, M. 2023. Manga Pilgrimages: Visualizing the Sacred/Sacralizing the Visual in Japanese Junrei. In *Comics, Culture, and Religion: Faith Imagined*, ed. K. De Groot, pp. 147–68. London: Bloomsbury Academic.

Mairesse, F. 2019. The Definition of the Museum: History and Issues. *Museum International* 71(1–2): 152–9.

Manning, P. 2017. No Ruins. No Ghosts. *Preternature* 6(1): 63–92.

Mathieu, C. 2003. *A History and Anthropological Study of the Ancient Kingdoms of the Sino-Tibetan Borderland – Naxi and Mosuo*. New York: Edwin Mellen Press.

Mauss, M. 1979[1950]. The Notion of Body Techniques. In *Sociology and Psychology: Essays*, trans. B. Brewster, pp. 97–119. Boston, MA: Routledge and Kegan Paul.

McDougall, D. 2016. *Engaging with Strangers: Love and Violence in the Rural Solomon Islands*. New York: Berghahn Books.

Mchunu, K. 2020. Roadside Death Memorials Revisited: Mourning in Public Spaces. *Cogent Arts & Humanities* 7: 1792154.

McKhann, C. F. 1992. Fleshing out the Bones: Kinship and Cosmology in Naxi Religion. Ph.D. diss., University of Chicago.

McKhann, C. F. 2010. Naxi Religion in the Age of Tourism: Persistence and (Re)creation. In *Faiths on Display: Religion, Tourism, and the Chinese State*, ed. T. Oakes and D. S. Sutton, pp. 183–210. Lanham, MD: Rowman & Littlefield.

Minucciani, V. 2013. Considerations in Relation to the Museography for Objects of a Religious Nature. In *Religion and Museums: Immaterial and Material Heritage*, ed. V. Minucciani, pp. 11–23. Turin: Umberto Allemandi & C.

Moore, R. 2009. *Understanding Jonestown and Peoples Temple*. Westport, CT: Praeger.

Moore, R. 2011. The Stigmatized Deaths in Jonestown: Finding a Locus for Grief. *Death Studies* 35(1): 42–58.

Moore, R. 2021. A Monumental Problem: Memorializing the Jonestown Dead. In *Beyond the Veil: Reflexive Studies of Death and Dying*, ed. A. Thaman and K. M. Christodoulaki, pp. 187–207. New York: Berghahn Books.

Mu, L. 1995. *Reveal the Secrets of Dongba Culture*. Kunming: Yunnan People Publisher.

Nabobo-Baba, U. 2006. *Knowing and Learning: An Indigenous Fijian Approach*. Suva: Institute of Pacific Studies, University of the South Pacific.

Nakano, R. and Y. Zhu. 2020. Heritage as Soft Power: Japan and China in International Politics. *International Journal of Cultural Policy* 26(7): 869–81.

Nash, J. 2012. Re-Examining Ecological Aspects of Vrindavan Pilgrimage. In *Flows of Faith: Religious Reach and Community in Asia and the Pacific*, ed. L. Manderson, W. Smith, and M. Tomlinson, pp. 105–21. Dordrecht: Springer.

Nayacakalou, R. R. 1975. *Leadership in Fiji*. Melbourne: Oxford University Press.

Nyíri, P. 2006. *Scenic Spots: Chinese Tourism, the State, and Cultural Authority*. Seattle, WA: University of Washington Press.

Oakes, T. 1998. *Tourism and Modernity in China*. London: Routledge.

Obadia, L. 2015. When Virtuality Shapes Social Reality: Fake Cults and the Church of the Flying Spaghetti Monster. *Online – Heidelberg Journal of Religions on the Internet* 8: 115–28.

Obeyesekere, G. 1992. *The Apotheosis of Captain Cook: European Mythmaking in the Pacific*. Princeton, NJ: Princeton University Press.

Okamoto, T. 2014. Otaku Tourism and the Anime Pilgrimage Phenomenon in Japan. *Japan Forum* 27(1): 12–36.

O'Leary, S. D. 1996. Cyberspace as Sacred Space: Communicating Religion on Computer Networks. *Journal of the American Academy of Religion* LXIV(4): 781–808.

Olson, P. R. 2016. Knowing "Necro-Waste." *Social Epistemology* 30(3): 326–45.

Paine, C. 2013. *Religious Objects in Museums: Private Lives and Public Duties*. London: Bloomsbury Academic.

Picard, D. 2015. White Magic: An Anthropological Perspective on Value in Antarctic Tourism. *Tourist Studies* 15(3): 300–15.

Pimenova, K. 2022. Museums and Religious Heritage: Introduction. *Civilisations. Revue Internationale d'Anthropologie et de Sciences Humaines* 71: 13–28.

Preziosi, D. 2014. Myths of Nationality. In *National Museums: New Studies from All Around the World*, ed. S. J. Knell, P. Aronsson, and A. B. Amundsen, pp. 55–66. London: Routledge.

Qian, F. 2009. Let the Dead Be Remembered: Interpretation of the Nanjing Massacre Memorial. In *Places of Pain and Shame: Dealing with "Difficult Heritage,"* ed. W. Logan and K. Reeves, pp. 17–33. Abingdon: Routledge.

Radermacher, M. 2021. "Not a Church Anymore": The Deconsecration and Conversion of the Dominican Church in Münster (Westphalia, Germany). *Material Religion* 17(1): 1–28.

Reader, I. 2005. *Making Pilgrimages: Meaning and Practice in Shikoku*. Honolulu, HI: University of Hawai'i Press.

Rees, H. 2000. *Echoes of History: Naxi Music in Modern China*. New York: Oxford University Press.

Reinarz, J. 2014. *Past Scents: Historical Perspectives on Smell*. Urbana, IL: University of Illinois Press.

Robbins, J. 2004. *Becoming Sinners: Christianity and Moral Torment in a Papua New Guinea Society*. Berkeley, CA: University of California Press.

Rock, J. F. 1947. *The Ancient Na-Khi Kingdom of Southwest China*, vol. 1. Cambridge, MA: Harvard University Press.

Ryde, J. 2009. Church or Museum? The Case of Santa Croce, Florence, Italy. *The International Journal of the Inclusive Museum* 2(2): 39–50.

Sahlins, M. 1985. *Islands of History*. Chicago, IL: University of Chicago Press.

Sahlins, M. 1992. The Economics of Develop-Man in the Pacific. *Res* 21: 12–25.

Sahlins, M. 1995. *How "Natives" Think: About Captain Cook, For Example*. Chicago, IL: University of Chicago Press.

Schieffelin, E. L. 1985. Performance and the Cultural Construction of Reality. *American Ethnologist* 12(4): 707–24.

Schroeder, R., N. Heather, and R. M. Lee. 1998. The Sacred and the Virtual: Religion in Multi-User Virtual Reality. *Journal of Computer-Mediated Communication* 4(2): JCMC425.

Scott, M. W. 2007. *The Severed Snake: Matrilineages, Making Place, and a Melanesian Christianity in Southeast Solomon Islands*. Durham, NC: Carolina Academic Press.

Scott, M. W. 2016. To Be Makiran Is to See Like Mr Parrot: The Anthropology of Wonder in Solomon Islands. *Journal of the Royal Anthropological Institute* 22(3): 474–95.

Shenar, G. 2019. Indian-Jewish Shrine Hopping in Israel: The "Multisensoriality" of Religiously Defined Practice, Emotion, and Belief. *Journeys* 20(1): 98–129.

Singleton, A. and M. Tomlinson. 2025. *Let the Dead Speak: Spiritualism in Australia*. Manchester: Manchester University Press.

Sissons, J. 2014. *The Polynesian Iconoclasm: Religious Revolution and the Seasonality of Power*. New York: Berghahn Books.

Smith, J. Z. 1987. *To Take Place: Toward Theory in Ritual*. Chicago, IL: University of Chicago Press.

Spicer, A. 2006. "God Will Have a House": Defining Sacred Space and Rites of Consecration in Early Seventeenth-Century England. In *Defining the Holy: Sacred Space in Medieval and Early Modern Europe*, ed. A. Spicer and S. Hamilton, pp. 207–30. London: Routledge.

Stafford, C. 2010. The Punishment of Ethical Behavior. In *Ordinary Ethics: Anthropology, Language, and Action*, ed. M. Lambek, pp. 187–206. New York: Fordham University Press.

Stasch, R. 2016. Dramas of Otherness: "First Contact" Tourism in New Guinea. *HAU* 6(3): 7–27.

Stokes, D. and L. Dearsley. 1981. *More Voices in My Ear*. London: Futura.

Storm, S., ed. 1969. *Philosophy of Silver Birch*. Oxshott: The Spiritual Truth Press.

Su, X. and P. Teo. 2009. *The Politics of Heritage Tourism in China: A View from Lijiang*. London: Routledge.

Swaffer, H. 1962[1947]. *My Talks with the Dead*. London: Spiritualist Press.

Teaiwa, K. M. 2015. *Consuming Ocean Island: Stories of People and Phosphate from Banaba*. Bloomington, IN: Indiana University Press.

Teeger, C. and V. Vinitzky-Seroussi. 2007. Controlling for Consensus: Commemorating Apartheid in South Africa. *Symbolic Interaction* 30(1): 57–78.

Tengan, T. P. K. 2016. The Mana of Kū: Indigenous Nationhood, Masculinity and Authority in Hawai'i. In *New Mana: Transformations of a Classic Concept in Pacific Languages and Cultures*, ed. M. Tomlinson and T. P. K. Tengan, pp. 55–75. Canberra: ANU Press.

Tofaeono, A. 2000. *Eco-Theology*: Aiga – *The Household of Life; A Perspective from Living Myths and Traditions of Samoa*. Erlangen: Erlanger Verlag für Mission und Ökumene.

Tomlinson, M. 2009. *In God's Image: The Metaculture of Fijian Christianity*. Berkeley, CA: University of California Press.

Tomlinson, M. 2014. *Ritual Textuality: Pattern and Motion in Performance.* New York: Oxford University Press.

Tomlinson, M. 2017. Try the Spirits: Power Encounters and Anti-Wonder in Christian Missions. *Journal of Religious and Political Practice* 3(3): 168–82.

Tomlinson, M. and T. P. K. Tengan, eds. 2016. *New Mana: Transformations of a Classic Concept in Pacific Languages and Cultures.* Canberra: ANU Press.

Verdery, K. 1999. *The Political Lives of Dead Bodies: Reburial and Postsocialist Change.* New York: Columbia University Press.

Viejo-Rose, D. 2011. Memorial Functions: Intent, Impact and the Right to Remember. *Memory Studies* 4(4): 465–80.

Vilaça, A. 2005. Chronically Unstable Bodies: Reflections on Amazonian Corporalities. *Journal of the Royal Anthropological Institute* 11(3): 445–64.

Vilaça, A. 2016. *Praying and Preying: Christianity in Indigenous Amazonia.* Berkeley, CA: University of California Press.

Violi, P. 2012. Educating for Nationhood: A Semiotic Reading of the Memorial Hall for Victims of the Nanjing Massacre by Japanese Invaders. *Journal of Educational Media, Memory, and Society* 4(2): 41–68.

Wagner, R. 2012. *Godwired: Religion, Ritual and Virtual Reality.* Abingdon: Routledge.

Wagner, R. 2014. This is Not a Game: Violent Video Games, Sacred Space, and Ritual. *Iowa Journal of Cultural Studies* 15(1): 12–35.

Wallis, R. J. 2012. Pagans in Place, from Stonehenge to Seahenge: "Sacred" Archaeological Monuments and Artefacts in Britain. In *Art, Faith and Place in East Anglia: From Prehistory to the Present*, ed. T. A. Heslop, E. Mellings, and M. Thøfner, pp. 273–86. Woodbridge: Boydell and Brewer.

Warden, I. 2013. Thoughts on a Labyrinth. *Canberra Times*, www.canberratimes.com.au/story/6161892/thoughts-on-a-labyrinth/, accessed August 26, 2024.

Wicker, C. 2003. *Lily Dale: The Town That Talks to the Dead.* New York: HarperOne.

Willis, M. 2015. Detritus to Treasure: Memory, Metonymy, and the Museum. In *Sacred Objects in Secular Spaces: Exhibiting Asian Religions in Museums*, ed. B. M. Sullivan, pp. 145–52. London: Bloomsbury.

Winter, J. 2006. *Remembering War: The Great War between Memory and History in the Twentieth Century.* New Haven, CT: Yale University Press.

Woolgar, C. M. 2006. *The Senses in Late Medieval England.* New Haven, CT: Yale University Press.

Xu, D. 2023. Tibetan Elements in Spirit Names in Dongbaism and Dabaism. In *Personal Names and Naming from an Anthropological-Linguistic Perspective*, ed. S. Ndlovu, pp. 189–216. Berlin: De Gruyter Gmbh.

Yamamura, T. 2014. Contents Tourism and Local Community Response: Lucky Star and Collaborative Anime-Induced Tourism in Washimiya. *Japan Forum* 27(1): 59–81.

Yamamura, T. and P. Seaton, eds. 2020. *Contents Tourism and Pop Culture Fandom: Transnational Tourist Experiences*. Bristol: Channel View.

Yang, F. 2008. *Ethnographic Papers of Yang Fuquan on the Naxi Ethnic Group*. Beijing: China Books.

Zengin, A. 2019. The Afterlife of Gender: Sovereignty, Intimacy, and Muslim Funerals of Transgender People in Turkey. *Cultural Anthropology* 34(1): 78–102.

Zhu, Y. 2012. Performing Heritage: Rethinking Authenticity in Tourism. *Annals of Tourism Research* 39(3): 1495–513.

Zhu, Y. 2018. *Heritage and Romantic Consumption in China*. Amsterdam: Amsterdam University Press.

Zhu, Y. 2022. Hot Interpretations of Difficult Heritage: The Memorial Hall of the Nanjing Massacre in China. *Journal of Cultural Heritage Management and Sustainable Development* 12(1): 32–44.

Zhu, Y. and N. Li. 2013. Groping for Stones to Cross the River: Governing Heritage in Emei. In *Cultural Heritage Politics in China*, ed. T. Blumenfield and H. Silverman, pp. 51–71. New York: Springer.

Zhu, Y., S-L. Wang, and M. Rowlands. 2020. Heritage and Religion in East Asia. In *Heritage and Religion in East Asia*, ed. S-L. Wang, M. Rowlands, and Y. Zhu, pp. 1–12. Abingdon: Routledge.

Zwigenberg, R. 2014. *Hiroshima: The Origins of Global Memory Culture*. Cambridge: Cambridge University Press.

Cambridge Elements ≡

New Religious Movements

Founding Editor
†James R. Lewis
Wuhan University

The late James R. Lewis was a Professor of Philosophy at Wuhan University, China. He was the author or co-author of 128 articles and reference book entries, and editor or co-editor of 50 books. He was also the general editor for the *Alternative Spirituality and Religion Review* and served as the associate editor for the *Journal of Religion and Violence*. His prolific publications include *The Cambridge Companion to Religion and Terrorism* (Cambridge University Press 2017) and *Falun Gong: Spiritual Warfare and Martyrdom* (Cambridge University Press 2018).

Series Editor
Rebecca Moore
San Diego State University

Rebecca Moore is Emerita Professor of Religious Studies at San Diego State University. She has written and edited numerous books and articles on Peoples Temple and the Jonestown tragedy. Publications include *Beyond Brainwashing: Perspectives on Cultic Violence* (Cambridge University Press 2018) and *Peoples Temple and Jonestown in the Twenty-First Century* (Cambridge University Press 2022). She is reviews editor for *Nova Religio*, the quarterly journal on new and emergent religions published by the University of Pennsylvania Press.

About the Series

Elements in New Religious Movements go beyond cult stereotypes and popular prejudices to present new religions and their adherents in a scholarly and engaging manner. Case studies of individual groups, such as Transcendental Meditation and Scientology, provide in-depth consideration of some of the most well known, and controversial, groups. Thematic examinations of women, children, science, technology, and other topics focus on specific issues unique to these groups. Historical analyses locate new religions in specific religious, social, political, and cultural contexts. These examinations demonstrate why some groups exist in tension with the wider society and why others live peaceably in the mainstream. The series highlights the differences, as well as the similarities, within this great variety of religious expressions. To discuss contributing to this series please contact Professor Moore.

Cambridge Elements

New Religious Movements

Elements in the Series

Black Hebrew Israelites
Michael T. Miller

Anticultism in France: Scientology, Religious Freedom, and the Future of New and Minority Religions
Donald A. Westbrook

The Production of Entheogenic Communities in the United States
Brad Stoddard

Managing Religion and Religious Changes in Iran: A Socio-Legal Analysis
Sajjad Adeliyan Tous and James T. Richardson

Children in New Religious Movements
Sanja Nilsson

The Sacred Force of Star Wars Jedi
William Sims Bainbridge

Mormonism
Matthew Bowman

Jehovah's Witnesses
Jolene Chu and Ollimatti Peltonen

Wearing Their Faith: New Religious Movements, Dress, and Fashion in America
Lynn S. Neal

J. Krishnamurti: Self-Inquiry, Awakening, and Transformation
Constance A. Jones

Santa Muerte Devotion: Vulnerability, Protection, Intimacy
Wil G. Pansters

Making Places Sacred: New Articulations of Place and Power
Matt Tomlinson and Yujie Zhu

A full series listing is available at: www.cambridge.org/ENRM

For EU product safety concerns, contact us at Calle de José Abascal, 56–1°, 28003 Madrid, Spain or eugpsr@cambridge.org.

www.ingramcontent.com/pod-product-compliance
Lightning Source LLC
LaVergne TN
LVHW020352260326
834688LV00045B/1678